Therapeutic Conversations with Queer Youth

Therapeutic Conversations with Queer Youth

Transcending Homonormativity and Constructing Preferred Identities

Julie Tilsen, PhD

JASON ARONSON
Lanham • Boulder • New York • Toronto • Plymouth, UK

Published by Jason Aronson
A wholly owned subsidiary of The Rowman & Littlefield Publishing Group, Inc.
4501 Forbes Boulevard, Suite 200, Lanham, Maryland 20706
www.rowman.com

10 Thornbury Road, Plymouth PL6 7PP, United Kingdom

British Library Cataloguing in Publication Information Available

Library of Congress Cataloging-in-Publication Data

Tilsen, Julie Beth, 1962–
Therapeutic conversations with queer youth : transcending homonormativity and constructing preferred identities/Julie Tilsen.
p. ; cm.
Includes bibliographical references and index.
ISBN 978-0-7657-0978-3 (cloth : alk. paper)—ISBN 978-0-7657-0979-0 (ebook)
I. Title. [DNLM: 1. Homosexuality—psychology. 2. Adolescent. 3. Bisexuality—psychology. 4. Gender Identity. 5. Transsexualism—psychology. WM 611]
616.85'83—dc23
2013000481
ISBN 978-1-4422-4779-6 (pbk: alk, paper)

™ The paper used in this publication meets the minimum requirements of American National Standard for Information Sciences Permanence of Paper for Printed Library Materials, ANSI/NISO Z39.48-1992.

Printed in the United States of America

Contents

Foreword

Therapeutic Conversations with Queer Youth: Transcending Homonormativity and Constructing Preferred Identities explores the question of how queer youth construct and perform queer identities within a homonormative context. In this volume, Julie Tilsen provides both conceptual and practical groundwork for the renewal and reconstruction of professional practices as they relate to working with queer youth. Tilsen does much more than make a major contribution to the existing literature on youth identity construction, queer theory, and the helping professions; she pushes beyond existing literature and offers, with her engaging and clarifying prose, new forms of understanding in our work with queer youth.

Specifically, her collaborative work with the Q-Squad offers readers much more than access to their voices; it offers a set of resources and practices that are at the heart of a relational constructionist philosophical stance and queer theory. Simply put, the partnership between Julie and the Q-Squad sits at the center of constructing, deconstructing, and reconstructing queer youth identities. The understanding that identity is always under construction and can only momentarily be located in any given category is central to this work. To that end, this volume moves us beyond the normative discourse of LGBT identities and opens a space where professionals and youth can actively construct and reconstruct multiple identities and thus generate performative possibilities.

As colleagues, we have enormous admiration for the commitment and coherence of Julie's work—and, that commitment and coherence is amply on display in this volume. Just as postmodern approaches to therapy and social services avoid "knowing about" the people with whom we work, this volume avoids "talking about" youth and instead is focused on "talking with" youth. In her writing, as much as in her practice, Julie Tilsen has seamlessly integrated the complexity of queer theory, social construction, and postmodern practices.

Those who teach courses on diversity and multicultural issues know how challenging it can be to avoid reifying stereotypes of various marginalized groups, particularly when discussing gay and lesbian identity and experience(s). In addition to ignoring the lived experiences of bisexual, transgender, and intersex persons, the majority of therapeutic, social work, and social service literatures and pedagogies on sexuality are informed by a reductionist, traditional gay and lesbian identity development model; in principle, a linear "coming-out" model. This conventional model is considerably restraining. Certainly, on one hand, a model that privileges "identity" does provide important meaning for many. Yet, this model, informed by the modernist notion of a fixed, linear, and essential identity, often leads to a premature foreclosing of lived experiences of countless sexual and gender minorities. This is certainly the case with the experiences of so many queer-identified youth who refuse to be reduced to fixed identity categories and conventional social markers. To be sure, we are using *queer* in the same way that Julie Tilsen uses it—not as an umbrella term, but as a political way of being that critiques the limitations of identity. Most of these queer youth feel erased or marginalized by the mainstream LGBT community due to their intentional refusal to assimilate to mainstream identity categories and ways of being, or what Julie refers to as "homonormativity." From their vantage point, sexuality and gender categories may be useful but are equally policing and regulatory. Yet, there is virtually nothing in the social work and orthodox gay and lesbian literature that speaks to their experiences of the limitations and problems of identity politics.

Just as the embodied experiences of queer youth do, queer theory—with its acute skepticism of identity categories and binary understandings of sex and gender—offers an alternative to the traditional gay and lesbian identity developmental paradigm. I (DN) was fortunate to be exposed to queer theory in my doctoral program in cultural studies at the University of California, Davis. Queer theory has been fairly widespread and commonplace in sociology, woman and gender studies, cultural studies, and literature and history, but has been virtually ignored by the academic and applied worlds of psychology, social work, counseling, and family therapy. This is both interesting and troubling, because queer theory is a creative and rich complement to social constructionist ways of working with clients due to its focus on language, meaning, and deconstructing normative discourses. Queer theory offers conceptual and theoretical tools to unhinge binary meanings of sex and gender that allow clinicians to honor queer clients and their radical and multiple identities. Consequently, queer theory in action helps us break from limiting and specifying identity conclusions, bringing forth generative therapeutic outcomes.

So, given its potentiality, why hasn't queer theory found its way into the psychotherapy field? Perhaps the main reason is that queer theory has been understandably critiqued for its elitist academic, dense, and obfuscating language that can ignore the material, social, and institutional conditions within which sex and gender minorities live. It can be rather difficult to translate the ideas of queer theory into actual and practical therapeutic applications. There is a disconnect between queer theory in the academy and the "real" world of therapy. However, it doesn't have to be that way! That is where *Therapeutic Conversations with Queer Youth* comes to the rescue as it makes this important link.

Julie Tilsen, with her innovative theoretical insights and practical case examples, in partnership with her consultants—the Q-Squad and their local knowledges—offers us new ways of thinking that disrupt conventional therapeutic ideology and provide a fresh therapeutic landscape for practitioners. However, caution is advised: Dr. Tilsen asks readers to sit with some discomfort around our taken for granted assumptions of sex and gender identity (even those of us who identify as "liberal"!). But it's well worth it—Julie and the Q-Squad offer us the resources not only to revolutionize and radicalize therapy but also to pave a path to a much larger social project that may unleash us from contemporary understandings of sexuality and gender.

David Nylund, PhD, Sacramento, California
Sheila McNamee, PhD, Durham, New Hampshire

Acknowledgments

No road is long with good company.

—Turkish proverb

Somehow I've managed to gather along the road that led to this book, so much amazingly good company, I have to pinch myself.

Everyone should have in their life at least one person with the intellectual dexterity, relational wisdom, wicked-smart sense of humor, and unrelenting commitment to social justice that each of these folks have. These friends and colleagues provided support ranging from razor-sharp feedback to big warm fuzzies: Kristen Benson, Dennis Dion, Ken Hardy, Stephen Madigan, Brier Miller, Scott Miller, Gerald Monk, Murilo Moscheta, Ottar Ness, Jennifer Sampson, and John Winslade.

Thank you to my editor, Amy King, and Jason Aronson for supporting this book project.

A special shout-out to Dan and his crew at Butter Bakery and Café in Minneapolis for keeping me warm, fed, and caffeinated with local, organic, sustainable, and delish noshes as I occupied hours on end of your cozy space in my neighborhood. Thanks for making community.

To my agent Scott Edelstein—I can't imagine doing this without your measured guidance . . . and off-the-wall humor.

Thanks to longtime friend Emily Scribner-O'Pray for sharing your great knowledge of youth sexuality with me.

Dave Nylund and Sheila McNamee did so much more than cowrite a most fabulous foreword. Your patinas are peppered throughout this book, and go well beyond my frequent referencing of your critical scholarship. Simply put, this book doesn't happen without either of you. The voices of my internalized Dave and internalized Sheila provide never-ending creative ideas, reassuring comfort, and much-needed encouragement.

How do I properly acknowledge and sufficiently thank the scores of clients who have shared such deeply personal and hugely consequential conversations with me over the years? Therapy is a tricky thing, dialogically poking around in people's lives. Writing about it even more so. My best effort is to constantly remind myself—and to ask those around me to remind me when I've failed to do so—how precious and privileged it is to be included in people's lives in this way.

I have been forever changed by the powerful and delightful conversations I had with the Q-Squad: Sarah Dack, Mateo Llanillos, Ruben Llanillos, Dylan Ralke, and Courtney Slobogian. Your individual and collective passions, commitment, and love—for each other, our conversations, and ideas—carried me through this book project. Now I carry our discussions—your voices resonating in my mind's ear—into every conversation I have with or about queer youth. I'm down for another inquiry project made from love and critical thinking (with a side of curry and a pitcher of beer) if you guys are—you in??

Finally, there would be no book without my partner Lauri. Hey babe—my MacBook won't be coming to the North Shore with us anymore. Just my hiking boots. Let's hit the trail and continue this amazing adventure we started in 1994. Thanks for making the space for me to write this book and for your tremendous and often-unsung contributions toward making the world a better place for queer youth. You rock.

Introduction

Queering Your Practice or Practicing Queer?

Q: *What are you wanting people who read this book to come away with after reading your words?*
A: *That they'll take it seriously.*

—Sarah, Q-Squad member

This book is written for therapists who question (or want to) prevailing assumptions, who dare to (or want to) doubt sacred cows, who do (or want to) believe our work is about justice, and who do (or want to) experience the work as more productive and meaningful when we know that we *really don't know*. Much of what informs our work as therapists hinges on cultural and theoretical assumptions that don't account for all the ways that people move through the world. They also don't necessarily provide the best way forward.

I don't intend this to be another therapist how-to book, although it does include reflective exercises, case examples, conceptual frameworks, and conversational resources for practice—all stuff that can be quite useful in the development of therapeutic know-how and skill.

Perhaps I should say I don't intend this to be *only* a how-to book. Part application, part reflective practice, part introduction to queer theory, and part critical cultural analysis, this volume was written, in part, because I believe therapists need an analysis in order to practice ethically—I know that I do.

I did not say that therapists need to *be in analysis*—I said that they need to *have* an analysis—that is, a critical, situated, and deconstructed understanding of the politics and power relations inherent in the culture and the work.

As you read this book, you will deepen your analysis and sharpen your ability to translate that depth of understanding into practice.

Why write about *homonormativity* and practice? In 2008 I was asked to coauthor[1] a chapter about working with queer youth for a book. I was interested in writing about homonormativity and exploring with queer youth their experiences with this regulating discourse. This interest emerged from my professional and personal experiences as well as from my interest in queer theory.

I was increasingly personally frustrated with the use of "queer" by people as a sort of umbrella term for the alphabet soup, "LGBTTQQI2"[2] (among the many iterations that exist) understanding it as a "taking back" of a pejorative term (as some African Americans intend with "the N word"). I desired a more intentional, critical use of the word *queer*—one that honored its destabilizing discursive potential for fluidity and its critique of identity politics. Such a use of the word *queer* would also show due respect for the importance that the words *gay*, *lesbian*, and *bisexual* have in many people's lives. These are identities that, for many people, have personal and political meaning that play a significant part in how they move through the world, affording them what many would call "agency." *Queer* does not resonate with, nor is it meaningful to—in fact, it may be quite distasteful to—many who do prefer to identify with a fixed and stable L/G/B/T identity. It is a very unqueer ethic to tag someone with something they don't accept or prefer.

My professional interest in exploring homonormativity grew in part from my work with queer clients and students. Many, especially younger people, were reporting the effects of not only heteronormativity (i.e., compulsory and assumed heterosexuality, heterosexual privilege and bias, homophobia, and the imposition of the gender binary) but also of being policed by other LGBTTQQI2 people. Some were told they were "too gay." Others were told they weren't "gay enough." Transgender clients and students who sought to embrace a fluid, genderqueer, androgynous, or otherwise multigendered identity described running into what I've come to call *transnormativity*. They were often challenged by trans individuals who preferred to "pass" as male or female and who found a place for themselves within a binary system. I also heard from clients and students the ways in which the prevailing discourses of contemporary *gay* culture were specifying and unwelcoming of their identities, sexual ethics, gender presentations, and broader political critiques of their world.

At the same time, I was aware that the literature[3] on working with LGBTTQQI2 clients was informed—at best—by a critical multicultural perspective that included attention to intersectionality. The notion of "gay affirmative" practice has entered the professional lexicon. This is certainly useful in communicating that overt heterosexism is not the intended practice and that one's LGBTTQQI2 identity will be embraced, not pathologized or ignored. Yet, the literature and these practices are not always explicitly inclusive of *queer* identities (except when using queer as an umbrella term) nor do they tap into the provocative and valuable resource that is queer theory. And, while the concept of *heteronormativity* is showing up more and more in the practice literature, one is hard-pressed to find a treatment of *homonormativity* outside of queer theory and other critical disciplines (despite Duggan's initial coining of the term back in 2002).

The book you have in your hands takes up an issue in homonormativity that is sorely lacking in the practice literature, and sadly present in the lives of queer youth.

BRIDGING THE WORLDS OF THEORY, PRACTICE, AND LIVED EXPERIENCES

Consideration of homonormativity, especially in the lives of queer youth, is not the only thing that has been missing from the practice literature. A world of conceptual frameworks in the social sciences has gone largely untapped in the applied fields. Counseling psychology, family therapy, and clinical social work are influenced overwhelmingly by modernist ideas of identity development. Therapists learn to conceptualize people from the limited (and limiting) offerings of practice literature informed by psychologized accounts of human experience. Our practices continue to be influenced by philosophies and theories that emerged at a cultural moment that was unprepared to account for the existence of contemporary queer youth. While we as practitioners have stood still, scholars, researchers, and activists from queer studies, cultural studies, gender studies, communication, anthropology, ethnic studies, and sociology (among other disciplines) have forged ahead, generating a wealth of theories and methodologies that can open up the floodgates of possibility in clinical practice.

What are the consequences of this? Limited by the accepted discourses of Western psychology, therapists working with queer youth have often unwittingly functioned in ways that are unsupportive of their identity constitutions. This occurs when we rely on essentialist theories of homosexual identity development based on modernist psychological notions of the "self" that insist on a self-contained, fixed, stable identity. This theoretical foundation (and the practices that emerge from it) exist at odds with the relational and fluid understandings of identity held by many queer youth.

Inasmuch as "gay affirmative" therapy relies on essentialist and psychologized accounts of identity, it fails to capture the constructionist ethos and political intentionality that help to define queer subjectivities. This failure creates a chasm of theoretical and ethical significance, the latter of which can have devastating repercussions on queer youth when we fail to hear them, see them, or understand them on their terms.

At the epicenter of this chasm is the clash of modernist and postmodern accounts of the self, which will be addressed in chapter 2. Modernist ideas have established hegemonic status throughout North American culture. They serve as the ideological foundation not only for psychological theories that inform practice, but also for the readily available, avidly consumed, pop psychology offspring of these theories.

The gap between the world of the practitioner and the world of queer youth exists in two discursive frames: "academic literacies" (Chiseri-Strater, 1991) and insider knowledges and lived experiences (Welle, Fuller, Maul, & Clatts, 2006).

In this book, I define *academic literacies* as the ideas from queer theory and social construction that proliferate within the academy in the social sciences, and in interdisciplinary areas of critical inquiry such as gender studies, anthropology, and sociology. While this knowledge is generated in the academy, it rarely crosses over into applied fields (e.g., psychology, social work, family therapy). Even when it does, it typically loses its theoretical rigor and integrity. It is presented in bits and pieces, incoherently situated within modernist discourses, and inconsistently applied in ways that subvert the subversive nature of its original intent.

Insider knowledge refers to the understandings and expertise that are gained from being positioned within, and obtaining experience from, being part of a particular community (Anderson & Burney, 2004). This includes the ways in which queer youth think about, talk about, and make sense of their queerness. Insider knowledge stands in contrast to so-called "expert" knowledge. While we may recognize concepts from queer theory, social construction, and other critical bodies of scholarship in insiders' personal accounts, insider knowledge is born out of lived experiences. This knowledge evolves experientially, reflects idiographic qualities, and often challenges conventional, "expert," academic and theoretical understandings.

As you read, you will find insider knowledge presented in two ways. First, you will hear from several clients I have worked with over the years.[4] The voices of these youth and their families are presented as case vignettes. These are intended as practical resources. I invite you to consider how you can put into practice the ideas presented in these vignettes. Second, you will read comments from five different youth—Courtney, Dylan, Mateo, Ruben, and Sarah—throughout. This group of queer youth served as my cultural consultants as I wrote this book. A more thorough introduction to these five, collectively known as "The Q-Squad," follows. The conversations with the Q-Squad members can be read as examples of queer-theory informed practice, even though we did not meet to "do therapy."

By bridging the gap that exists between current practice and the subjective accounts of queer youth, a radical new path can be forged for therapists and their clients. This path—born in conversation, skeptical of specifications, honoring of transgressions, intrigued by possibilities, committed to justice, and embodied in relationship—opens up conversational space that is welcoming and generative of a proliferation of identity constructions.

This path also deconstructs and critiques the modernist notion of *identity development* and introduces the postmodern notion of *identity construction*. This perspective is informed by queer theory, social construction, and, most significantly, the lived experiences of queer youth: how many queer youth think about who they are, talk about who they are, and aspire to be in the world.

The material that follows may leave you spinning—in (I hope) a good and productive way. You will reflect on what you thought you knew about youth and identity, gender and sexuality, systems of power, and how language works. Certainly my own introduction to social construction and queer theory had that effect on me. It also deeply reenergized me and recommitted me to my practice.

They also paved the way to alternative practices that have helped me to stay contextual, flexible, and responsive. They opened up many new pathways of meaning for my clients and me. In addition, the emphases on constructed and fluid identities helped me refocus on *therapy as social construction* (McNamee, 2004), in which engaging in conversation with clients is a generative process, "meaning is on the move" (McNamee, personal communication, May 20, 2011), and we embrace the productive potential of uncertainty.

INTRODUCING THE Q-SQUAD

Throughout this volume, you will hear from the Q-Squad: five youth who served as cultural consultants to this book. Their comments, excerpted from six meetings spanning three months, provide insider knowledge that anchors this work in the lived experiences of queer youth. Our conversations focused (more or less) on how they thought about queer identity and their experiences with therapists.

Below is a brief introduction—in their own words—to each of the participants, all of whom were unequivocal about wanting to be identified in this work, thus underscoring that *claiming* their voices is as important as *having* a voice.[5]

Sarah Dack and Courtney Slobogian:[6] Youthful post-homo lipstick enthusiasts with white privilege in their knapsacks, queer in their hearts, and academia in their brains. Both work extremely hard to bridge the gaps in between.

Mateo Llanillos: Ruben's twenty-three-year-old brother. Born in Nicaragua and raised in Winnipeg, Manitoba, Mateo identifies as a queer trans male.

Ruben Llanillos: Age nineteen, genderqueer, Hispanic. Mateo Llanillos is my older brother. I like wearing fur during inappropriate occasions and enjoy writing in cursive. I am an artist.

Dylan Ralke: Option 1: Your run of the mill, twenty-something, flask-in-the-bag, young professional. A mishmash of your typical cross-country European background, but with a heart that burns with the passion of Canadiana. Queer and questioning, prep and punk. Never quite on one side or the other, but always stuck in the middle. *Option 2:* Twenty-three-year-old, male identified, strawberry blonde, hazel-eyed Ukrainian. Queer, yet always questioning. Bored and serious young professional by day. Eccentric and loud un-professional by night.

As for myself, I go through the world with the wind at my back for the most part: white, middle-aged, American, educated, (currently) able-bodied, cisgender,[7] middle-class, professional. As a queer-identified, secular Jewish woman, I also occupy social locations that are marginalized to varying degrees in varying contexts. Coming to these conversations with the Q-Squad, I remained cognizant of ways in which my age, class, and position as a professional represent privilege and authority with young people.

DON'T SKIP THE HARD STUFF: HOW TO READ THIS BOOK

I have written this book in at least two voices: my academic/theoretical/scholarly voice and my conversational voice used for telling stories from the field and engaging in personal reflection. This was both organic and intentional. Sometimes there is a deliberate blurring or blending of these voices. Writing in this way came without thinking about it. Among the stories I tell, I imagine you may hear different voices as well.

I am similarly conversationally and relationally responsive and flexible in my therapy practice. I "show up" in different ways—and with different voices—from client to client and sometimes from session to session with the same client.

Multiple voices and identities are also key concepts of social construction and queer theory. One of my gripes about the field of psychotherapy is that there exists an estrangement (*can we get a relationship therapist in here, please?*) between those that engage in scholarly activities and practitioners. As we will see, social construction and queer theory challenge binaries such as the scholar/practitioner divide. This book is meant to be accessible *and* challenging, informative *and* engaging. Please don't skip the hard stuff.

A glossary follows. The terms and concepts are central to this book. While they will be defined and discussed in greater length as they are applied throughout the text, it is important to review them up front.

Chapters 1, 2, and 3 provide the conceptual foundations and definitions required to read the rest of the book. *Chapter 1* explores therapist positioning and ethics. This is also where you will find a discussion of the Q-Squad, how their conversations informed this book, and how working with them reflects the ideas and practices described throughout the book. *Chapter 2* provides an overview of social construction. *Chapter 3* introduces queer theory, defines some relevant terms and concepts, and maps out the ways in which these areas of scholarship can strengthen our therapeutic practice with queer youth.

Chapter 4 offers a critique of models of homosexual identity development, including queer theory critiques of the conventional discourse around "coming out" and the notion that we are born this way.

A queer-constructionist treatment of youth sexuality is the subject of *chapter 5*. This chapter also confronts the paucity of sex-positive information available for *any* youth, and provides therapists with resources that invite supportive and respectful conversations that make the previously unmentionable mentionable.

Chapter 6 introduces cultural studies frameworks that facilitate productive conversations about youth's consumption of popular and media culture.

Chapter 7 discusses violence and other products of unrestrained prejudice. It offers suggestions for practice and action beyond the walls of the therapy office.

In *chapter 8* the Q-Squad offers observations on how to keep the queer in queer and how to avoid fixing what is meant to remain fluid.

Throughout the book you will find questions for reflection. These are offered to encourage deconstruction and meaning-making and, I hope, the raising and investigation of some questions of your own. You may want to consider these questions with a colleague, with your clinical supervisor, or in conversation with yourself, a friend, or a client.

Throughout this book you'll read case examples of work I have done (or encountered in supervising other therapists' work) with queer youth and their families. These are not definitive, cookbook, how-to examples. Each case represents one way of deploying the resources discussed in this book, one way that worked at one moment in time.

Please accept this as my invitation to rethink, reimagine, remember, and reclaim your practice in a way that is relationally responsive and socially just. It's an invitation to queer your practice—not based on *who or what* you see, but on *how* you see.

NOTES

1. Tilsen, J. & Nylund D. (2010). Homonormativity and Queer Youth Resistance: Reversing the Reverse Discourse. In L. Moon (Ed.) *Counselling ideologies: Queer challenges to heteronormativity* (pp. 93–104). London: Ashgate Publishing.
2. Lesbian, gay, bisexual, transgender, transexual, queer, questioning, intersex, and 2 spirit.
3. Across disciplines within counselor education, psychology, family therapy, clinical social work, and youth work.
4. All identifying information has been changed to protect privacy. Also, it has always been my practice ethic to only write about clients who have given me explicit permission to use their stories. Where that is not possible, I have created composites of several different client stories compiled from my practice as a therapist and the practices of those I supervise or consult.
5. Parker (2005) discusses the notion of "anonymity" in research, providing a useful argument for reconsidering this practice.
6. Sarah and Courtney wrote their bios together. This, itself, is a queering of traditional practices of writing bios and introducing oneself individually rather than relationally.
7. Cisgender is a term that describes people who identify with the gender that they were assigned at birth.

Glossary

A new word is like a fresh seed sown on the ground of the discussion.
—Ludwig Wittgenstein, philosopher

Binary

Within structuralism, binary oppositions are central organizers of language and cultural/social activities. Two related ideas are defined against each other; each is defined by what it is not. For example, the idea that there are two genders, woman and man, represents the gender binary.

Cisgender

Cisgender is a term used to describe people who identify with the gender they were assigned at birth. It is opposite of transgender (*cis* being the prefix meaning "on the same side" and *trans* being the prefix "on the opposite side"). In some queer and transgender activist communities, describing someone as cisgender is preferred to previous descriptions such as, "non-transgender" or "biological" male/female. Using *cisgender* and *transgender* challenges the dominant practice of naming only identities that occupy marginalized positions (e.g., black, gay, disabled, etc.), thus implying that identities that go un-named (e.g., white, straight, able-bodied, etc.) are the standard or norm. Also, using both transgender and cisgender makes visible the experience of gender for everyone.

Deconstruction

A process used to understand text (words, concepts, etc.) in context and to expose taken-for-granted assumptions embedded within. Deconstruction operates on the assumption that nothing exists outside of text; no objective reality has meaning outside of the context(s) that gives it meaning. For example, gender identity disorder (GID) is a diagnosis used today. However, throughout history and across cultures, there have existed people who express and embody a variety of genders. These people were not diagnosed or labeled in such a way. In fact, in some cultures they held special spiritual or healing status. Through the process of deconstruction, we can see how GID and, indeed, all expressions of gender, gain meaning within the contexts from which they emerge.

Discourse

Discourse is what gets to be said, who gets to say it, and with what authority. Foucault (1970) defines discourse as a "social practice" that circulates through culture. Discourse has a regulating effect on what may or may not be spoken. We cannot speak, think, feel, or act in a way that is free from the influence of discourse. Even resistance and transgressions gain their meaning through their relationship to discourse. Examples of influential discourses include: capitalism, patriarchy, individualism, and psychiatry/psychology.

Discursive

Discursive is the adjective form of discourse. It describes the contexts in which all language and social activity occur. Thus, it gives meaning to individual experiences. For example, the discursive context produced by the gender binary (that is, the ways we speak about gender and the assumptions we make about it and how we value it, etc.) gives meaning to terms such as *male* and *female*. In therapy practice, discursive approaches examine the ways in which cultural meanings are produced and understood. A discursive therapeutic approach emphasizes the constructionist perspective that language produces meaning.

Essentialism

Essentialism asserts that specific core (or "essential") characteristics or properties are shared by all members of a particular group regardless of context. Common essentialisms include: men are naturally aggressive and all youth go through the same developmental stages.

Hegemony

The dominating position of a social group (and their ideas and practices) over others, to the degree that these ideas and practices gain normative status as "truth." For example, in North America, the values and assumptions that emerge from white, middle-class, heterosexual family structures have hegemonic status.

Heteronormativity

Heteronormativity is the institutionalized assumption that everyone is (or should be) heterosexual and that heterosexuality is inherently superior and preferable to any orientations outside of heterosexuality.

Homonormativity

Homonormativity mimics heteronormativity by embracing many of the same values and assumptions of domestic, heterosexual institutions and consumer consumption. These shared values and assumptions include: the privileging of a fixed and stable sexual identity; a privatized and domesticated version of sex; focus on nuclear familial arrangements; and middle-class lifestyle and values. By mimicking heteronormativity, homonormativity creates a binary opposition to heteronormativity, thus reifying the dominance of the former rather than generating a proliferation of other possible ways of being. It invokes a politics of sameness or assimilation rather than one of resistance and transgression. An example of this is seen in the efforts to repeal "Don't Ask Don't Tell" rather than challenging militarization and participation in war.

Individualism

Individualism, as used in this book, refers to one way, albeit the dominant way in Western culture, of understanding people and how they engage in social activities. Individualism assumes that people are self-contained beings and that inside of our bodies all of our characteristics, attributes, thoughts, feelings, etc., exist independent from those of other people. It is related to *essentialism* and stands in contrast to *social construction.*

Modernism

Modernist philosophy is a product of the Enlightenment. It features the search for universal truths to explain all human experience and adherence to the empirical methodologies used in the natural sciences to discover these truths or ostensibly universal and objective realities.

Normativity

In the social sciences, normativity describes cultural prescriptions and proscriptions that specify and regulate social activity, generally shaping these activities toward homogeneity.

Performativity

From a constructionist perspective, identity is said to be *performative*, that is, a kind of performance that is realized through repetition of language and other social activities. Performance is not about "acting" or "pretending"; rather, it stands in juxtaposition to the essential self that is cast as "authentic," "true," "natural," and self-contained in the modernist discourse of individualism. For example, gender is said to be performative because ideas about how to be a man or a woman are produced by and circulated through language, and regulated through the discourse of the gender binary.

Postmodern

Postmodern philosophy maintains that realities and knowledge are historically and culturally contingent. Thus we cannot make claims of universality. Further, the process of knowledge production and discovery is central to the knowledge itself and cannot be separated from it.

Poststructuralism

Poststructuralism emerged as a critique of the fundamental assumptions of structuralism (see below). It rejects totalizing, essentialist accounts of subjectivity and the centrality of binary opposition. Rather than understanding underlying structures to hold the real meaning of things, poststructualism understands all things to be productions contingent on discourse. For example, gender is not viewed as a static characteristic (i.e., structure) that exists "in" people that has a universally shared meaning. Instead, it is understood to be produced through language and circulated through discourse, gaining meaning within the discursive context from which it emerges.

Queer

Queer serves as a critique of identities, rather than as an identity constitution of its own, and stands in resistance to fixed identity categories. It is not used in this book as an umbrella term for LGBT, although it has come to be used that way by others. Here, it is a signifier that stands against "normal" and in defiance of any and all categories.

Social Construction

A philosophical stance that focuses on language practices (what occurs between people) rather than a focus on the observation of objects (what is ostensibly inside of people). Social constructionist philosophy stands in opposition to individualism and essentialism.

Structuralism

Central to structuralism is the notion that each thing has a basic structure that constitutes its realness, regardless of relationship and context, and that we can know this structure through observation.

Text/Story/Narrative

Within social construction, postmodernism, and poststructualism, the concepts of text, story, and/or narrative are used as the organizing metaphors for understanding people's lives and how they make meaning of them. The narrative metaphor holds on to the idea that people make meaning of their lives in relation to others and to the contextual influences they encounter; meaning is not "hard wired" in us at birth, nor is it "out there" waiting for us to discover it.

Chapter One

Where Do You Stand?

Queer Ethos and Accountability

The engaged voice must never be fixed and absolute but always changing, always evolving in dialogue with a world beyond itself.

—bell hooks, author and activist

I really like reading how my experiences fit into a different framework, something bigger than me.

—Sarah, Q-Squad member

How might your practice change if you decenter professional knowledge about youth identity, sexuality, and gender by privileging the knowledge that queer youth hold about these matters?

What conclusions (and nonconclusions) may emerge in your work with clients if you develop a situated understanding of sexuality and how it becomes imbued with meaning by locating it in history and culture?

What reactions, judgments, feelings, and beliefs may become unhinged if you understand the politics of constituting one's identity—including your own—based on *who someone has sex with?*

What cultural or professional discourses that influence your work would become open to reconsideration if you were to sincerely—not in a token manner—center the opinions, meanings, and actions of young people?

Who might you become as a practitioner if you came to unknow much of what we are trained to be quite certain about?

These are the questions I asked myself when, many years ago, I first found that I was really listening to the stories of queer youth. Their lives were evidence that much of what I took for granted was not an inclusive account of how people move through the world. While I sat in conversations with them, an epiphany resonated with me loudly and clearly: liberatory stories were buried in their accounts of struggle. Bringing those stories of resistance and agency out from the margins helped me, and continues to help me, generate answers to those questions. It also continues to lead to more questions, which is always important. Otherwise, I fall into the trap of being too sure about something or otherwise close off the path to new possibilities. Despite being a questionmonger, I have had to pull myself up and dust myself off many times after being tripped up by the call of certainty.

Indeed, any book about anything *queer* is about exploding certainty and provoking questions. It is about fluidity rather than fixity, creating rather than consuming, truths rather than Truth, and imagining rather than replicating.

This is a book for therapists who want to resist the enticement of certainty and venture into the complexity and possibilities—as well as the challenges and struggles—inherent in the worlds of queer youth. It's also for therapists who seek to interrogate not only what often goes uninvestigated in the culture at large, but also so-called truths of psychological theories and practices that we are taught to adhere to with great fidelity, and even reverence.

In this chapter, I will discuss ideas of therapist positioning (Davies & Harre, 1990) as a matter of ethics and accountability and the principles that guide my therapeutic work. I will also describe how these principles inform my relational ethic and how I used them in the research and writing of this book.

My partnership with the five queer youth who comprised the Q-Squad is a reflection of this ethic, and also serves as an illustration of relationally engaged, queer-theory informed work with youth.

> *You're still just two people sitting in a room, engaging, right? The therapist is bringing themselves to that.*
>
> —Courtney, Q-Squad member

THERAPIST POSITIONING: A MATTER OF ETHICS

We affect people's lives. How we position ourselves with others—from the language we use, to the examples we draw on, to how we think about who they are (and why they are that way) and how we think about who we are (and why we are that way)—is an ethical choice.

By *positioning* I mean a number of things, all of which have to do with the way you situate yourself in relationship to clients and to the cultural institutions and discourses that influence your relationship and work with them. As Harre and Van Langenhove (1999) point out, "The rights for self-positioning and other-positioning are unequally distributed and not all situations allow . . . for an intentional positioning" by all participants.

Because of this unequal distribution, when working with queer youth it is incumbent upon us to recognize the power and authority we have. This authority comes from being positioned culturally as adults and professionally as therapists. Recognizing and accounting for these privileges can help us choose a relational stance that positions queer youth as competent agents who can speak with authority about their lives.

For example, we can choose to position ourselves in a way that invites rich, contextualized stories, creating discursive space for queer youth to "bring all of themselves" to the conversation. As an adult professional, this would be a practice of accountability, a way to decenter (but not dismiss) ourselves within the conversation. Conversely, we can choose to position ourselves in ways that privilege the institutional authority we carry. Unfortunately, many of the theories that inform our work and the practices we rely on often have the effect of shutting down space for queer youth rather than opening it up.

Positioning contributes to how we define ourselves *in that conversational moment within the relationship at hand.* Are we, for example, positioning ourselves as expert or as unsure, as authoritative or as curious, in charge or in partnership? No one position is the right position; indeed, from a constructionist perspective, we are interested in finding a positioning that is the best fit and that moves the conversation in a direction that is most productive and meaningful to our clients.

Furthermore, in a conversation, when we position ourselves, we also position our conversational partner(s). When we consider this notion alongside the cultural authority and privilege we have as adults and therapists in youth's lives (and I'm not even factoring in matters of social location and cross-cultural counseling issues), the ethical significance of how we position ourselves is clear.

Below are some questions for reflection about positioning in your practice:

1. *How do you think of yourself in relationship to your clients, and your clients in relationship to you?*

   For example, do you assume a position of expert authority? Do you see yourself as equal to your clients? As collaborators? What does this mean? How do you conceptualize and explain your professional position and power? Is this consistent or does it depend on the client? How do you decide? What about self-disclosure? Do you think that clients are the only ones changed/inspired/provoked/touched by therapy, or do you expect to be changed by, and learn from clients, as well? Many therapists have a metaphor that reflects their view of themselves in relationship to their clients. What's your metaphor? What does that suggest about your positioning?

2. *How do you think about the purpose of your relationship?*

   What's your job? What's the client's job? What are the intentions in meeting together? How do you define what you are doing? What are the results, outcomes, by-products of this relationship? What are the implications (meanings and effects) of your thoughts about this?

3. *How do you think about your relationship with external institutions of authority (e.g., licensing boards, professional guilds, third-party payers, corrections, social service systems, medical authorities, etc.)?*

   Whom do you work for and account to? What authorities (individual and institutional) do you turn to for information and direction in your practice? How do you feel about and use DSM diagnoses? Do you contract with insurance companies? How do you communicate with and share information with collateral service providers? How do you talk about clients with others?

4. *In work with minors, how do you think about your relationship with them and with the adults involved in their lives?*

   Who is/are your client(s)? Whom do you work for? How do you communicate about the young person with the adults? How do you talk about the adults with the young person? How do you manage multiple perspectives?

5. *How do you think of yourself in relationship to prevailing cultural discourses?*

   In what ways do you consider the impact of your social location on your identity as a therapist, and in relationship to the social location of your client? Do you think of the process of therapy as being immune from cultural discourses and local politics? In what ways do you explore prevailing discourses and their effects on you, your clients, and your work?

6. *How do you decide to communicate (or not communicate) to your clients the ways in which you view all of these relationships?*

   What are your thoughts about transparency? How do you understand it as different from self-disclosure? What are the ethical and practice implications of your stance on transparency?

These questions are intended to facilitate your reflection on the ethical issues of positioning and accountability, two concepts that get tossed around frequently among therapists, but often do not receive close consideration.

It is important to begin this book with this brief consideration of positioning because intentional and deliberate focus on positioning permeates this work—from the research, to the writing, to the choice of theoretical resources, to the clinical practices described herein. Social construction and queer theory, the two major theoretical streams that we will dive into in the following chapters, demand a positioning that departs radically from conventional ideas. I invite you to continue to reflect on and take note of the positioning choices that are implicitly or explicitly described throughout the book.

QUEER THEORY, RELATIONALLY ENGAGED WRITING

Because this is a book about therapeutic applications of queer theory and social construction with queer youth, I wanted to engage in a writing process that would be philosophically consonant with both a constructionist and a queer ethos. In addition to writing in multiple voices, I invited a group of queer youth to serve as my cultural consultants. In doing research for this book, I wanted to be accountable to and inclusive of the queer lives of the youth I would be writing about. In seeking this consultation, I sought to position their insider knowledge side by side with scholars and theorists. In short, I am saying to you, "I want you to take these guys seriously."

By placing their comments alongside theoretical arguments, I hope to bring forward the relationship between theory and lived experience, and to demonstrate how two discursive frames can articulate the same concepts very differently.

There were some 150 pages of transcript from our meetings; I included comments that stood out for me as particularly poignant, provocative, and/or representative of an idea or perspective that may not otherwise be available to many practitioners. I also included Q-Squaders' observations that brought to life the process of relationally engaged identity construction.

Finally, in my efforts to privilege queer youth, decenter expert knowledge, work toward accountability, and queer the writing process, I took one step further: I invited the youth who participated in the Q-Squad to write reflections and responses to what I've written. This affords them the proverbial last word. It also extends the conversation in both content and process, furthering the generation of ideas. Additionally, the inclusion of queer youth's writing destabilizes (in a useful way) traditional notions of research and writing that privilege so-called expert knowledge. Thus, it's a pretty queer practice.

Two of the members of the Q-Squad, Courtney and Sarah, offered written responses to two of the chapters. Here is what they together wrote about why they did this:

> When Julie approached us to "write into" her book the two of us . . . both felt a strong sense of connection to the idea of engaging with academic ideas from a new space. . . . Making our academic understanding applicable and present in

> our lived experience seemed to be possible through this work. Participating in this work has helped us to create a space where we see our academic lives and our lived experience interacting. Meeting with Julie and the rest of the group, as well as reflecting on this experience and Julie's writing has helped the two of us [to] intentionally bring that space forward in a meaningful way.

While the other Q-Squaders chose not to write responses to my written material, they all had access to the transcripts of our meetings and had the chance to clarify verbally, expand on, or change anything that had previously been discussed.

These acts stand in opposition to many traditional writing and research practices that situate "subjects" more as objects and position the writer as sole authority. This practice is also philosophically consistent with the relational tenets of social construction. And, of course, it embraces a queer politics of resisting norms. In short, I queered my writing and research process.

To *queer* something is an emergent process of disrupting expected norms in such a way that new possibilities emerge and standard, unquestioned practices become open for interrogation.

Constructionist philosophy advocates for multiple perspectives and the centering of local or insider knowledge. Queer theory (situated within the broader spectrum of poststructural theory) provides us with theoretical resources to engage in critical practices that disrupt convention. In the case of this book, this includes deconstructing conventions around "professionalism" related to research and writing. I need to make these behind-the-scenes processes visible here because the ethic behind them is central to the core ideas of this book.

In all of my work—from research to writing to therapy to teaching—I intend to center the experiences and voices of those involved (in this case, queer youth) as much as possible.

The following practices embody this stance and relational ethic:

- *Accountability to relations of power*. This means treating my conversational partners as experts in their lives and ensuring space for the performance of their knowledge. My commitment to upholding this value is informed, in part, by Foucault's (1978a, 1978b) critique of knowledge production based on systems of discipline and punishment. By attending to the power relations inherent in my conversations with youth, I engage with them in ways that resist or avoid disciplinary or confessional practices.
- *Transparency*. This involves sharing my "in-my-head" conversations with my clients, situating my ideas and questions, and telling them about my ideas, plans, thoughts, and purposes. Transparency is by definition, dis-

tinct from *self-disclosure*. Transparency is about making the conversational and relational process (and what I am experiencing within that process) visible and available to others so that they may not only understand the process, but also influence it.
- *Self-Reflexivity*. Parker (2005) describes this as "enthusiastic self-questioning rather than fanatical certainty" (p. 21). This means contextualizing and examining what's going on with me so I can make accountable decisions about the work and in my relationships with others.
- *Responsiveness*. This means that I am providing respectful, relevant, non-tokenizing responses to those I'm working with. I respect, respond to, and act on their preferences, perspectives, and interests.
- *Social poetics and conversational imagination*. By allowing the process to unfold without the overimposition of particular methods, models, or theories, I make space for a proliferation of identity performances, new knowledge, and emergent meanings. McNamee (2000) observes that, "to talk of the poetic is to give wing to the imaginative" (p. 146).

Critical to these ethics is a decentering (but not a denial) of expert knowledge in order to bring forward knowledge of participants. In the case of this book, my conversations with the Q-Squad were immeasurably valuable to my understanding of queer youth and to my ability to write about my clinical work in a way that is anchored to real lives.

As you read the following chapters, I hope that you will see theory and lived experience as mutually generative and as partners in creating meaningful lives.

Chapter Two

Social Construction

I Was Discursively Produced This Way

What's present is having the awareness to know that when I encounter a person I can't pretend to know anything about them. Holding on to the fact that really I know nothing about anyone, right? I think everyone looks for signs that we can recognize or figure out things about someone but just holding on to the fact that even if I make an assumption, I'm probably wrong, and that's okay.

—Courtney, Q-Squad member

How do we go on?

—Ludwig Wittgenstein, philosopher

Social construction is a philosophical stance that is an important shift away from modernist assumptions about the world. These assumptions have effectively served as Western culture's guiding metanarrative since their emergence during the Enlightenment. Gergen (1985) notes that social construction is "concerned with explicating the processes by which people come to describe, explain, or otherwise account for the world (including themselves) in which they live" (p. 266). The primary distinction between modernism and social construction involves the shift from a focus on objects to an emphasis on language practices. Through the constructionist lens, we are able to consider that many assumptions about our world are produced and maintained through discourse (Foucault, 1970).[1]

For example, certain discourses specify what sorts of behavior are considered appropriate at work. As a North American, such discourses produced by and for the maintenance of a neoliberal capitalist culture tell me that I need to maximize "productivity," which is defined as billable hours. I'm to limit my time socializing with colleagues and engaging in activities that cannot readily be understood as generating capital.

When I visited professionals working in similar settings in Aotearoa/New Zealand,[2] I found that they worked under a different discourse, one that bore the mark of Maori and Pacific Island cultures. In these cultures, time spent "socializing" and eating at work with colleagues was considered to be productive. In fact, not to do so, to "keep your nose to the grindstone," would be unprofessional and rude, because relationships carried value that in my American context do not. Consequently, my assumptions about how to conduct myself as a professional became exposed as situated meanings influenced by particular discourses.

As a way of understanding how people make sense of their lives, constructionists also focus on the performative use of language and the production of reality through discursive practices (Guanaes & Rasera, 2006). This view of language shifts from the modernist emphasis on the individual—in which language is seen as a representation of reality—to the social activities shared between people—who then became agents of the production of reality (Wittgenstein, 1953).

Many theoretical traditions fall under the rubric of social construction. I will touch on a variety of influences that are located within this broad camp of ideas; however, my main emphasis will be on those that are informed by poststructural theory (Derrida, 1967, 1977; Foucault, 1965, 1970, 1973, 1977, 1978a, 1978b).[3] I made this decision because of the relationship between queer theory (the primary theoretical resource of this book) and poststructural ideas. Also, I am a narrative-trained therapist, and the theoretical underpinnings of narrative therapy come from the poststructural camp. (However, I take care to regularly question my narrative training and its own taken-for-granted assumptions.)

Fundamental to social construction is a skeptical view toward knowledge. In part, this involves questioning not only *what* we know, but also *how* we came to know it, and *who* such knowledge might privilege. For example, the physical act of sex is generally viewed as "natural." When we understand things to be "natural," we assume their universality as well as their stability. Foucault (1978a, 1985), Rubin (1984), and Tiefer (2004) discuss the historical and cultural contingency of sex, noting that ideas such as "homosexuality" and "bisexuality," as well as specific behaviors that are understood to constitute sex in a contemporary Western context, are unknown in other places. Sexual essentialism, which views sex as natural, and as existing before and independent of social relationship, is an artifact of Western medical discourse, a prevailing discourse in our contemporary culture. (The discourses that produce and maintain notions of *sexual identity* will be discussed at length in chapter 4.) While biology is a necessary aspect of human sexuality, it is not sufficient. As Rubin (1984) remarks, "The belly's hunger gives no clues as to the complexities of cuisine" (p. 276). Thus, social construction does not reject or deny corporeal realities. It does, however, question the privileged position of scientific discourse, while also highlighting that nothing, including science, goes unmediated by culture.

The skepticism of social construction is practiced through deconstruction (Derrida, 1967, 1977). Deconstruction allows us to make visible the relationship among language, knowledge, and the contexts in which they exist. Rejecting the existence of singular and absolute "truths," Derrida proposed deconstruction as a way to illuminate fissures and inconsistencies in particular renderings of reality or knowledge by exposing their contextual contingencies.

We can ask deconstructive questions about sex in order to unhinge the certainty of its natural constitution, and, thus, to learn much about the contingency of meaning and its relationship to discourse. For example:

- *Has the definition of sex remained stable across time and in all places?*
- *Is the understanding of what constitutes sex stable across time and circumstances for each individual, or might that constitution change in a person's lifetime?*
- *Trace the meaning you have made of sex throughout your lifetime. What has stayed the same; what has changed? What circumstances influenced the various constitutions that you have embraced?*
- *Where do these understandings come from? Who had the authority to create these definitions?*
- *What influences impact what we as a culture agree to understand to be sex? How have media, religion, technology, the medical profession, and consumerism influenced current cultural understandings of sex?*
- *Whom does this particular meaning of sex include? Whom does it exclude?*
- *What does this idea of sex imply about other ideas of sex? For whose benefit does this idea of sex exist? Who pays the price of this idea of sex?*
- *How has your own experience of sex been similar to and different from what you read about, have seen in films, and learned in sex education? Which version is less "natural" than others?*
- *What might it mean that some people consider certain things to count as sex, while some people don't consider those things to be sex? How does this kind of variation in perspectives affect the assertion that sex is natural?*
- *If sex is natural, why do we have sex education?*

Thus de-essentialized and situated contextually, what had passed as "natural" or "immutable" becomes open to consideration and located within discourse. We see the possibility that other realities may be created out of other contexts, for other purposes, and by other agents of meaning production. We also see the process through which a particular construction—in this case "sex"—becomes reified through language and institutional practices such as heteronormativity, patriarchy, ableism, medicine, and consumer capitalism. Through deconstruction, social construction asks, "Why this construction, in this culture, at this time?" (Bohan et al., 1999, p. 16).

With a skeptical eye toward the production of knowledge, constructionists take up a radically different view of reality from modernists. Reality—everything we "know" about the world—is produced in language. All that we know is a byproduct of "communal interchange" (Gergen & Gergen, 2003, p. 2). This differs dramatically from the modernist discursive tradition which privileges individuals' capacity to reason, assumes that we can know with certitude, and uses language to convey these truths (McNamee, 1996a). Moreover, modernist constitutions of reality produce grand narratives and universal "truths" that transcend place and time. (Indeed, the modernist project is to *discover* explanations that can be universally assigned.) From a constructionist perspective, however, creating meaning is not a process of private interpretation engaged in by individuals. Nor is it a matter of observing and describing the "real world"; rather, it is an interactive social process that occurs within relationships and is mindful of discourse. Thus we shift from the notion that knowledge is discoverable ("the truth is out there") to the idea that knowledge is created. Knowledge is understood to be historically and culturally contingent, thus making context paramount to the production of meaning. Consequently, universal truths and grand narratives are rejected for local knowledge. Knowledge is made, not found (McNamee, 1996a).

In the questions above, for example, "sex" as "natural" is deconstructed. As such, we find that "sex" is not solely a biological function to be observed and described by medical science. That is *one* discursive frame that produces *one* particular reality of "sex." We also see that "sex" is constructed in a multiplicity of discourses. This leads to a proliferation of "realities," all dependent on context. Here, context includes when in history the knowledge was produced; the cultural influences on its production; and the position and agendas of the people involved in its production. Thus, a variety of discourses generate the "reality" of sex.

In a fundamentalist Christian discourse, for example, the reality of sex is very different than the reality created within the discourse of the critical disability movement.[4] Likewise, notions about sex that originate within hegemonic masculinity will stand in stark contrast to those emerging from third-wave feminist discourses. Here are some possible discursive statements that are products of—and are productive of—each of these discourses:

- *Fundamentalist discourse:* "Procreation is the purpose of marriage."

- *Critical disability discourse:* "All bodies are sexual bodies capable of giving and receiving pleasure."
- *Hegemonic masculinity discourse:* "Dude, if you don't nail her now, you are so gay."
- *Third-wave feminism discourse:* "If he gets to be a stud, I get to be a slut."

Whether we are sitting in church listening to a sermon, attending a poetry slam featuring disabled artists, downing beers at a sports bar, or reading *Bitch Magazine,* we are both influenced by and contributing to the production of discourse. While not always explicit, discourses are embedded within the language practices that we engage in. Operating as the assumptions requisite for making what we say or do legible to others, "discourse is the realm in which...what is 'real'...is constructed" (Monk, Winslade, & Sinclair, 2008).

Adopting these tenets of social construction requires us to abandon the representative view of language. In this view, language is believed to accurately describe reality, and reality is seen as something that can, in fact, be accurately described. Gergen (2009a) points out that the traditional view of language as descriptive is founded on the assumption that "truth can be carried by language" (p. 9), an assumption that renders some languages, and those that speak them, more "true" than others. Indeed, Shotter (2003) asserts that how we talk about our lives serves to "constitute and sustain one or another kind of social order" (p. 134). The "most true" language becomes the dominant discourse.[5]

The four statements above represent divergent discursive frames and clearly do not occupy the same position of influence and power. While many people may not subscribe to a fundamentalist Christian perspective of sex, the dominance of this discourse is visible in the lingering effects it has on contemporary American culture. Some of these include the legislative mandate for abstinence-only education, sodomy laws on the books until 2003, renewed culture wars in the political arena regarding birth control, and the pervasive assumption that "everyone" seeks (and should seek) a partner and wants (and should want) to be married and have children.

In their seminal work *The Social Construction of Reality: A Treatise in the Sociology of Knowledge*, Berger and Luckmann (1966) describe how the social production of knowledge and reality progresses from a contextualized local understanding to an institutionalized sedimentation of reality that "becomes real in an ever more massive way" (p. 59). Language serves as the vehicle of this process, fixing ideas and actions in time until they assume a reality status that is seemingly ahistorical, creating a "this is how it's always been" effect that goes unquestioned. As clinicians, we need look no further than the *Diagnostic and Statistical Manual of Mental Disorders* (DSM) (APA, 2000) to see how this process works.

Daily, we hear about "depression." Comments such as, "I'm depressed," "he's depressed," and "that's depressing" litter our conversations. There is no need to ask what is meant—we know, and we've always known. "Depression" has moved from the restricted domain of professionals to the daily discourse of laypeople, without question or skepticism. Yet, what is now codified as "major depressive disorder" in the current iteration of the DSM has a long history of name and criteria changes. These changes do not represent the outcomes of more precise and sophisticated scientific classification; rather, they are cultural artifacts, products of the medical and psychological zeitgeist of successive eras. Thus, the psychiatric "condition" commonly referred to today as "depression" is imbued with historical and cultural meaning, even if we've come to view it as an ahistorical, essential truth. This meaning serves as an emblem of its time and place, not to mention a badge for those with the authority to name it.

Yet it is important that we not create a binary opposition of modernism vs. social construction in the process of critique. Indeed, the above example of psychiatric diagnosis demonstrates how such a binary opposition is problematic. On one hand, modernist accounts of depression leave us with a decontextualized and static description of a person. This kind of description is reductionistic and totalizing, leading us to believe that we can know someone based on their diagnosis. We lose the curiosity necessary to inquire about alternative identities and acts of resistance that challenge depression as a meaningful description. On the other hand, because of the discursive culture we live in, without the currency of a diagnosis, many are unable to access appropriate services or have those services funded, often both.

Spivak's (1988) notion of strategic essentialism, defined as a "strategic use of positivist essentialism in a scrupulously visible political interest" (p. 205) offers a viable reworking of this dilemma. Spivak suggests that a critique of the limits and consequences of essentialized identity can be simultaneously acknowledged and temporarily suspended in order to leverage group identities (e.g., diagnostic categories) within political contexts (e.g., the medical hegemony). This is often necessary in order to access resources that are regulated through institutionalized power (e.g., the psycho-industrial complex, which includes big pharma, the insurance industry, psychiatric and other professional discourses, and governmental funding).

For example, transgender individuals seeking medical and surgical interventions must submit to what many consider highly oppressive medical and psychiatric regulation. This includes being diagnosed with so-called "gender identity disorder" and going through one year of "real life experience" (RLE) in the target gender. Thus, transidentified people who want to receive surgical interventions must first agree to a psychiatric diagnosis. Yet this diagnosis privatizes a social problem that is a result of the discursively produced gender binary system. Second, they must then take up a lifestyle that reifies that system and demands that they solidly "land" as either male or female, even if they prefer a more fluid expression. The question of who is granted the authority to determine which "real life experiences" constitute those of "men" and which constitute those of "women" further demonstrates the inherent dilemma. The choice to submit or not submit to these medicalized discourses and procedures is a false, humiliating, and painful choice for many. Yet they do so because of the political realities that dictate the terms of their existence in our culture.[6]

UNDOING INTERIORITY

In order to accept that meaning is relationally produced, constructionists must reject another firmly held assumption of modernism: the idea of the self contained individual. This assumption holds that a person's identity is determined by his or her *essence,* what is "inside." This essential self is understood to be fixed and stable. The hegemony of discourses that privilege essentialist notions of identity is readily visible in the use of clichés such as "authentic self," "true self," and "just be yourself." The prevailing cultural discourses of patriarchy and capitalism bear the mark of this notion of the self-contained, fixed, stable individual. Gergen (2009b) points out that, historically speaking, "the view of the individual as singular and separate, one whose abilities to think and feel are central to life, and whose capacity for voluntary action is prized" (p. xiv) is a product of the Enlightenment—that is, a construction as recent as three hundred years ago. Given its youth, we can't help but be struck by the strength with which this notion has taken hold.

Foucault (1965, 1973, 1977) contends that this modern invention of the individual has led to practices of objectification and subjugation through "dividing practices" (1965)[7] and "scientific classification" (1973).[8] These practices rely on the attribution of individual and social identities in order that regulatory regimes (the state, medicine, the prison system, et al.) may exercise social control. Furthermore, these practices establish the specification of the self-contained individual, which Foucault maintains is critical to the operations of power in the modern state.

Sampson (1989) also points to the ways that the self-contained individual exists in order to maintain modern power. He argues that North American psychology's allegiance to the notion of the self-contained individual is not evidence of the idea's validity as a "real" and "natural" fact; rather, psychology's focus on the self-contained individual simply serves to uphold the social structure. As a cultural artifact, psychology's view of subjectivity as a self-contained interiority "fits" with the "ongoing structures and arrangements of current Western society" (p. 3). To modify this view of self would require a wholesale paradigm shift. Sampson (1989) argues that the notion of a self-contained individual serves to uphold ideologies that reproduce a capitalist society, which in turn requires individuals committed to the reproduction of a self-contained interiority.

> *There are parts of the label that you attach yourself to but there are also parts of the label that you don't necessarily agree with . . . things that you don't agree with and so even though you may term yourself as something, you're always kind of resisting it . . . Like, I'm kind of, but at the same time, not really . . .*
>
> —Dylan, Q-Squad member

Given the limitations of the essentialist "self," constructionists prefer the term "identity." Unlike the fixity of the modernist "self," the notion of identity is preferred for its fluid and emergent qualities. Identity shifts through time and space and context, holding multiple possibilities for a proliferation of identity conclusions. While identity within a modernist framework is an object that can be clearly determined and understood as fixed and stable, constructionists hold that "identity becomes the accomplishment of situated activity" (McNamee, 1996b, p. 150). Relationships and the social discourses they embody are the situated activity. Thus, identity becomes both a *result* of relationships as well as an *antecedent* to relationships. Bakhtin (1986) suggests that our "self" would not be legible to others if it were not for the productive and recursive impact that relationships have. We acquire a "self" through the appropriation of the images that others hold of us. As Madigan (2008) puts it, "We are contributors to each other's identity" (p. 103). These contributions are situated within dominant discourses.

Deconstructed and thus de-essentialized, identity is exposed as an artifact of modernism. Thus, constructionists focus on relationship, or the discursive space between people as the site of identity production (Gergen, 2009a; Gergen & Gergen, 2003; McNamee, 1996a, 1996b). In this space, texts and embodied stories of self are constructed in relation to others.

For example, I have a long-standing story of myself as being "funny." I "know" this about myself—that is, how I have constructed this story about myself—through the stories my older siblings and my parents have told me over the years. Some of these stories I only know *as stories*; that is, the stories serve as my memory of the times my family recounts my being funny.[9] I have, in turn, told some of these very stories as examples of my long-standing identity as a funny person. Because of these stories, and the way in which people engage with me around them, I embraced being funny long ago. In eighth grade I was voted "best sense of humor" and in high school I was a candidate for that award. The story of me being funny generated stories about those stories. I came to embody funny. Those who know me helped to construct that embodied story about me, and they expect me to be funny in our relationships.

Embodied stories are a performance: we know how to "do" the identities that these stories script. How do we know how to perform these stories? Butler's (1990a, 1990b, 1993) notion of performativity, which developed from speech-act theory (for example, the work of John Searle, 1969), is relevant here. Performativity focuses on the ways in which identity comes to life through discourse. Performative acts are types of authoritative speech, speech that isn't merely representative but that *does* something. According to Butler (1990b), reality is constantly created "through language, gesture, and all manner of symbolic social sign" (p. 270). Through the embodied performance of identity and social conventions these constructions come to appear natural and immutable.

Key to performativity is repetition. My story about being funny gained its authority through its multiple tellings by multiple tellers. Also critical is the idea that "a performative is that discursive practice that enacts or produces that which it names" (Butler, 1993, p.13). This occurs only through its reference to, and reproduction of, the accepted norm. Thus, performance is not about "acting" or "pretending"; rather, it stands in juxtaposition to the essential self that is cast as "authentic," "true," and self-contained in modernist discourse. Performance accounts for the recursively productive relationships among individuals, their stories, and the discourses that give these stories meaning.

> *I started dating a boy. A friend that I hadn't seen for six months showed up one day and said, "I hear you're dating a boy." I was like, "I haven't seen you in six months—how'd you hear that? You've not been in the country." It was an enlightening moment: "I get it. I can't move in this space." It wasn't any different from being straight and feeling like I couldn't date a girl.*
>
> —Courtney, Q-Squad member

BEYOND TEXT TO DISCOURSE

The shift from essence to story frees us from the limitations of the self-contained interior. However, some argue that this shift still does not fully account for the effects of discourse. Queer theory contests the idea that individual texts alone can account for identity production (Butler, 1990a, 1997; Foucault, 1965, 1973, 1978b, 1982). Our personal stories gain meaning through their relationship to prevailing discourses. Thus, because of the institutionalized power of certain discourses, texts of identity are limited, and they are subject to the specifying and regulating effects of discourse. Indeed, queer youth must contend with multiple dominating discourses. How then, do we facilitate the transition from a focus on texts to an emphasis on discourse?

McNamee's (1996b) ideas may serve as a bridge between the two. Noting that "identity" as a concept is historically and culturally important (and I would add, pragmatically important as well, given that we all traffic in language), she suggests that we needn't abandon it altogether. Rather, we can adjust our relationship with it, viewing it not as an "entity" but a "conversational resource." By de-essentializing the term "identity," we can focus on "the way in which terms are used and the ways in which they gain significance in particular discursive contexts" (McNamee, 1996b, p. 151). Butler (1990a) makes the parallel observation that "the deconstruction of identity is not the deconstruction of politics; rather it establishes as political the very terms through which identity is articulated" (p. 189). Thus, "conversational resources" becomes a pliable concept, a politically situated construction of fluid identity.

Parker (1989) contends that texts are delimited areas that exist within the domain of wider cultural discourse, where as identity, or "the self," is "constructed in discourse and then re-experienced within all the texts of everyday life" (p. 56). Similarly, Butler (1990a) notes that daily social interaction is only part of discourse, which also encompasses texts, institutional practices, media representations, and law. Thus, while social construction points us to the daily interactions between people and the texts produced in those exchanges, a Foucauldian analysis broadens the view to include the dominating cultural narratives that shape and give meaning to the texts of individual lives—and what we call our identity. These constitutions of "self" are both influenced by and productive of cultural discourses and their normalizing specifications.

Consequently, Madigan (2008) asserts that our identities are "profoundly political," as we can only know ourselves within the context of normalizing discourses. As such, poststructural accounts of identity are greatly interested in the roles of both power and discourse in the shaping of identity categories. Indeed, social theorist Calhoun (as cited in Madigan, 2008, p. 103) maintains that "the fundamental reference of identity is a discourse in social location." Sampson (2008) concurs, pointing out that there is "no meaning independent of the cultural discourses which have engendered them in the first place" (p. 22) and noting that there is a close relationship between individual and cultural texts.

In short, because identities are produced within specifying dialogical structures, they cannot help but carry the influence of discourse. Identity is thus neither an independent product of a "natural" developmental process or a representation of an internal, essential self. In fact, Foucault argues that those very ideas are embodied by and in discourse.

Nor does identity emerge in unsituated social activity. Rather, identity is a product of discourse that regulates and polices what is available and acceptable, lest we incur societal sanctions (Shotter, 1989).

This centrality of discourse to the self reflects another principle undergirding constructionist philosophy: meaning is historically and culturally contingent. It is imperative that we recognize that guiding cultural narratives influence the individual meanings people make. Failure to do so is a failure to fully comprehend the discursive implications of constructionism and can effectively suck much of the meaning out of individual stories.

For example, when I embody funnyness as an instructor in front of a group of graduate students, discourses operate that specify what constitutes professional conduct for an instructor (as well as what is appropriate for a woman of my age and skin color); these discourses lend certain meanings to my performance of funny when I stand in the front of the classroom. These meanings differ from, say, those constructed by a group of friends when we sit around a campfire together and discourses of professional conduct do not apply. For some students, my performance might make me cool and my classroom fun; for others, I may seem like an unprofessional flake, leading them to question what I know and my ability to teach them. All of these meanings are produced within the crucible of my performance, their engagement with my performance as they perform their personal renditions of "student," and the various discourses that serve as constitutive backdrop.

Put simply, the move from modernism to social construction is a philosophical shift on a grand scale, and the implications and consequences are huge. When we reject universal truths for multiple realities and replace the self-contained individual with identity stories constructed discursively in relationship and situated within a multiplicity of discourses, we do many things. First, we unleash the potential for new and preferred identity conclusions, as identity is unhinged from the idea of a stable "essence." By exposing the specifying and regulating power regimes of dominating discourses, we allow ourselves to see identity performances that challenge these regulations as potentially honorable acts of resistance. We also allow ourselves to see and consider alternative, nondominating discourses in support of preferred identities. Finally, by acknowledging the relationship between individual stories and the discourses that they exist within, we avoid the burdens and limitations of individualism.

NOTES

1. Foucault (1970) defines discourse as a "social practice" that circulates through culture. Discourse has a regulating effect on what may or may not be spoken. We cannot speak, think, feel, or act free from the influence of discourse, as even resistance or transgressions gain their meaning through their relationship to discourse.

2. The agencies that welcomed my partner and me during a visit in 2004 included Taeomanimo Trust and Family Start in Porirua and The Family Centre and Hutt Valley Youth Health Service in Lower Hutt.

3. Poststructuralism emerged as a critique of the fundamental assumptions of structuralism as it rejects totalizing, essentialist accounts of subjectivity and the centrality of binary opposition. Poststructural ideas are used as a way of challenging dominant discourses and bringing forward subjugated knowledge.

4. Of course multiple discourses operate simultaneously and we all occupy social locations that place us, at times, in conflicting discourses. For example, someone who is influenced by fundamentalist Christian ideas of sex but who also, because of a disability, cannot reproduce, may question the fundamentalist notions when they are exposed to sex-positive attitudes in critical disability studies.

5. Dominant discourse refers to ideas embedded within cultural texts that have gained hegemonic status through reification and widespread reproduction of the ideologies, norms, and values from which they are constituted. They gain traction, in part, through authoritative endorsements from the realms of science, the academy, and/or law.

6. For an excellent analysis of the dilemma of the GID see Butler's 2006 essay, "Undiagnosing Gender."

7. Dividing practices are a method of objectification through social and spatial regulation that gains authority through the institutional power of science (or pseudoscience) and imposes specifying identities on individuals.

8. Scientific classification is another method of objectification that works by objectifying the body through the authority of the discourses of medicine or science.

9. For further reading on social constructionist ideas on memory, see Billig, 1990; Sampson, 2008; and Shotter, 1990.

Chapter Three

Queer Theory

The Audacity of Difference

I bumped into this guy I knew from a while ago and just kind of mentioned what we're doing here and he thought that queer was just a bunch of gay guys. He thought that I was just getting together with a bunch of young gay guys and hanging out. I had to explain to him what queer was to me, how I felt about it, and how I felt that we are trying to explain it and define it. It was just so interesting because he was a gay guy and he just assumed that I just meant other gay guys, that this was just a group of gay guys.

—Dylan, Q-Squad member

Being queer is not a matter of being gay . . . but rather being committed to challenging that which is perceived as normal. There is no foolproof membership criteria for queerness other than the willingness to seek out sites of resistance to normalcy in any possible location.

—Cathy Ruby, queer theorist

Many theoretical traditions exist within social construction. Queer theory, a term first enunciated by Teresa de Lauretis in 1991, offers constructionist-oriented practitioners a radical and challenging array of ideas and political strategies for working with identity, power, and relational ethics. While many theorists have contributed to the development of the body of scholarship that constitutes queer theory (for example, Butler, 1990a, 1993; Doty, 1993; Duggan, 2002; Foucault, 1978a; Halberstam, 1998; Rubin, 1984; Sedgwick, 1990, 1993; Warner, 1993, 1999), the work of Foucault (1978a) and Butler (1990a) have been particularly instrumental in the articulation of queer theory, its emphasis on the production of power, resistance as a central tenet of queer politics, and the role of discourse. Queer theory also owes much to feminist theory and its pioneering work in articulating the constructed nature of gender and the power relations produced within the gender system.

Central tenets of queer theory include a focus on de-essentializing cultural discourses; a Foucauldian analysis of power as productive and multidirectional; a view of identity as constructed, fluid, and culturally mediated; a politics that challenges normativity in all ways, especially the regulation of sex and gender; and sex positivity. For me, queer theory is a theoretical resource, an "intellectual tool" (Garber, 2003)—one of many I draw on.

Queer theory is firmly founded on anti-essentialist notions of identity. *Queer* itself is a "consequence of the constructionist problematizing of any allegedly universal term" (Jagose, 1996, p. 74) and an acknowledgment of the contingent nature of meaning. As an embodiment of the constructionist rejection of interiority and a fixed, unified identity, queer functions as a critique of identity (Halperin, 1997; Jagose, 1996; Warner, 1999), amounting to "an identity without an essence" (Halperin, 1997, p. 62). Furthermore, queer theory deploys the constructionist tenet that identity is relationally produced. As de Lauretis (1991) observes, "It takes two women, not one, to make a lesbian" (cited in Crimp, 1993, p. 313).[1]

Butler's (1990a) pioneering work, *Gender Trouble,* serves as another example of the constructionist ethic embedded within queer theory. Butler challenged feminists to acknowledge the socially constructed nature of the feminist argument that there are two biological sexes and that "women" constitute a unified constituency. Butler's work asserts a constructionist position in stating that no body is unmediated by culture. Thus, while not denying materiality, Butler insists that we remember that even the corporeal world—that is, its objects and their workings—is constructed discursively.

For example, no one would deny the materiality of a rock. Yet, how we talk about rocks certainly varies. In an angry playground fight, rocks might be weapons. In a solar home, rocks are a source of heat. In my garden, rocks are a nuisance. Our location, community, and traditions all shape meaning; the materiality of the world does not provide evidence against the discursive constructions of reality. Furthermore, Butler's notion of *performativity* (discussed earlier in chapter 2) has furthered the constructionist articulation of identity as nonessential and discursively produced.

Queer theory's primary focus is to complicate the hegemonic assumptions about the continuities between anatomical sex, gender identity, sexual identity, sexual object choice, and sexual practice. Challenging binary constructions—especially gender and sexual binaries—is of particular importance in queer theory. While constructionist discourse has promoted this practice and the de-essentializing of cultural truths, in the areas of sex and gender, the firm grip of naturalized accounts has been sadly evident, even in the constructionist literature.

For example, Mary Gergen (2003) seems blindly essentialist and firmly established within the male/female, homo/hetero binaries when she writes the following: "If He is the subject of the story, She must be the object" (p. 69) and when she reduces the options for personal stories to "manstories" and "womenstories" (p. 67). Similarly, Kenneth Gergen (1991), in an attempt to expose the limitations of the gender binary by discussing "transsexualism" (p. 144)—a term that focuses on a condition, a thing, rather than people and their lived experiences—reproduces the binary by conflating directionality (i.e., male to female) with identity and reifying the notion that each of us is either a man or woman. Furthermore, he relies on the work of Johns Hopkins researcher John Money, well known for falsifying research and for viewing "so-called social influences that impact on a person outside of biology" as the equivalent of astrology (Ehrhardt, 1991, xiii–xiv). The point here is not to engage in a full-on critique of Gergen's understanding of the gender systems or of his decision to reference someone reviled within genderqueer communities; rather, it is to highlight the extent to which naturalizing discourses of gender and sex influence the understanding and perspective of even ardent social constructionists. I also use this example to illustrate how queer theory, teetering at the edge of constructionist discourse, pushes the theoretical tradition—and the envelope—even further.

QUEER THEORY: OUT OF THE HEAD AND INTO THE EMBODIED[2]

Queer theory includes a range of critical practices premised on the poststructuralist notion of nonessentialized identities. Gender and sexual orientation are seen as fluid, socially constructed, contextually and historically contingent variables that shift and change in different contexts and at different times (Butler, 1990a). As a critical practice interested in interrogating the relationship among sex, gender, and sexual desire, queer theory situates these constructs within larger sociocultural contexts and explores the intersectionality with class and race, and the influence of consumer capitalism (Butler, 1990a; Foucault, 1978a; Halberstam, 2005; Sedgwick, 1990). Biological theories of sexual identity are rejected; prevailing assumptions regarding the continuities among anatomical sex, gender identity, sexual identity, sexual object choice, and sexual practice are complicated; the very usefulness of sexual and gender categories is questioned (Tilsen and Nylund, 2010).

In order to destabilize the discourses of "truth" and "nature" typically embedded within explanatory theories of gender and sexuality (not to mention within the theories and models promoted for clinical use), queer theorists ask the following questions about identity categories organized by gender and sexuality:

- *Whom do these categories serve?*
- *Whom do these categories include? Whom do they exclude?*
- *Who has the power to define the categories?*
- *How are the categories policed?*
- *How do these categories change over time and across cultures?* (Doty, 1993)

Central to queer theory's interrogation of these categories is the critique of the very premise of organizing one's identity based on group membership (McPhail, 2004). While such organization is politically useful at times, it is also problematic. Queer theory suggests that identity categories have reductionistic and totalizing effects. Particularly problematic in the production and effects of identity categories are the binary systems of gender and sexuality: female/male, homo/hetero. Butler (1990a) articulated the relationship between these systems of categorization like this: gender (one's sense of being a man or woman) follows from biological sex (assumed to be determined by primary sex organs); desire then follows "naturally" toward the opposite sex. Thus, Butler, argued, heterosexuality is both compulsory and naturalized, both regulated by and reifying of the gender binary system. Queer theory's challenges to the gender binary system calls into question the specifications of masculinity and femininity and leads to an unhinging of heterosexuality as the norm.

This kind of destabilization is culturally radical, especially within the fields influenced by psychology. Butler and Byrne (2008) note that traditional psychological theories and practices do not account for the notion of queer. Indeed, the binary systems described above go unquestioned by the "science" of psychology, as it assumes them to be internal attributes of individuals. Echoing Foucault (1988), Butler and Byrne observe that psychology is "involved in the production of knowledges that have served to reinforce the normalizing of heterosexuality and gender dichotomy and the oppression of other practices and identities'" (p.90).

The privatizing and pathologizing discourses of psychology are thus challenged by queer theory's position of "resistance and insubordination" (Hodges, 2008, p. 9) and its opposition to "normal" (Warner, 1999). Indeed, many queer theorists insist that resisting and disrupting any regulating and limiting discourses is an act of social justice.

> *For me it's about constantly trying to deconstruct things that are put in place to make people feel safe, like gender and sexuality. But it also applies to how people do relationships. I use it in a much broader context. I take queer and apply it to things outside of gender and sexuality to disrupt or deconstruct.*
>
> —Courtney, Q-Squad member

In my practice, I constantly reflect on how my cultural and professional training may keep me from being insubordinate to normalizing specifications and thus, encourage me to operate as an agent of social control rather than as a witness to meaningful acts of transgression. In fact, Foucault called for such insubordination:

> . . . the real political task in a society such as ours is to criticize the working of institutions which appear to be both neutral and independent; to criticize them in such a manner that the political violence which has always exercised itself obscurely through them will be unmasked, so that one can fight them. (As cited in Rabinow, 1984, p. 6)

How does one go about engaging in acts of insubordination toward the regulating discourses of psychology and the practice fields informed by those discourses? To begin with, we can understand the relationship between truth and power and how the discourses deployed by psychology are positioned as truth (by virtue of their ostensibly essential "scientific" nature). Foucault (1970) points out that when something is presented as truth, it increases in power and is seen as neutral. Yet, as we have seen, asking deconstructive questions about so-called "truths" can, in fact, reveal their contingent (and political) nature. Hence, resistance and insubordination start with asking questions about what we think we know and how we have come to know it. We can ask them of ourselves and in conversation with other practitioners, and we can reflect on them separately and together. We can ask questions that unhinge taken-for-granted organizational truths about the processes and procedures we put clients through (for example, intake forms, assessments, etc.). And we can ask questions about cultural institutions that instruct us in how we think and what we do. We can question the unquestionable.

In our practices, we can ask questions that help clients interrogate "truths" that hold them hostage to specifications that they cannot or prefer not to meet, yet by which they are judged under the gaze of normativity.

For example, I worked with a nineteen-year-old white cisgender[3] male, Max, who was attracted to cisgender women, had never had a sexual experience with another male, identified as straight, and was tormented by his erotic interest in cross-dressing and role-playing. He had a girlfriend who also identified as straight and whose only sexual experiences had been with straight men. Kim, also white and nineteen, was more than happy to participate in sexual play that involved his dressing as a woman and assuming "a passive position." For her, organizing around the idea of "being a good partner" had a lot of meaning, and part of that meant "being willing to try things that I am not opposed to for myself, that are enjoyable and exciting for him." I asked her, "In what ways is being 'straight' and being a 'woman' significant or not when you think about going along with these activities?"

Kim explained first that she saw "no harm, no foul" in Max's erotic interests, noting that he was always willing to indulge her pleasures. She went on to say that she didn't "know if being a straight woman really mattered—for me it's about what are we both okay doing that is sexy for either one of us."

I was taken by Kim's freedom from gender specifications and her positive embrace of sex (sex positivity will be discussed at greater length in chapter 5). When I asked Kim why she did not feel constrained by ideas of what's masculine, what's feminine, and what "normal" sex should look like, she explained that she hoped that "a sexual relationship would be one place that the people involved can try whatever they agree to and not have to do what we think we're supposed to do—I do that all day at work and school." She added, "frankly, being a 'good girl' isn't necessarily always the hottest thing, either."

Max listened to Kim in utter confusion. "I don't understand how she can be so cool with this. How can she not think I'm perverted or weird or something?" I asked Max questions that helped to unravel the grip of the gender binary, questions about hegemonic masculinity, and questions about sex and sexuality:

- *Who gets to decide what is normal sex—normal for a man and normal for a woman?*
- *What are the effects of these decrees of "normal" on people? Are all people affected equally by these judgments?*
- *In what ways do certain ideas about being a straight man influence your ideas about how to be sexual in your relationship?*
- *Can a straight male identity provide all the necessary or desired strategies for being the sexual person and partner you'd like to be?*
- *Does it feel like you are being punished for doing something that brings you and your partner such pleasure and meaning?*
- *Who might be behind this punishment and why do they think you should be punished?*
- *What ideas about gender and sex support this punishment?*
- *Is the pleasure that you and your partner experience a crime? Who are the victims?*
- *Would you say that it's possible you are being unjustly punished for a victimless crime?*
- *In what ways can you be a man that include so-called female qualities?*
- *In what ways are you a better man because of your ability to role-play being a woman?*
- *If you were to listen to your body instead of the rules of masculinity, how would that affect your sexual relationship? Other aspects of your relationship?*

- *What do you make of Kim, a woman, being turned on by your role-playing? What does that say about who owns masculinity and who owns femininity?*
- *Is it possible that your body's response to cross-dressing and role-playing is an honorable act of resistance to limiting ideas of "normal"?*

This kind of queer theory–informed interrogation of the gender binary helped Max and Kim organize their relationship around their values and preferences rather than prevailing discourses. Freed from the binary prescriptions of gender, they negotiated terms of a fluid gender performance between them. They queered themselves.

Furthermore, by challenging normative notions of the binary construction of sexuality, they were able to see sexuality as dynamic and fluid. Finally, by locating the problem within the discourses that sustain these binary systems, Max gained some room to consider how he wanted to move within these systems. This allowed him to embody the notion that he was a courageous transgressor of limiting cultural regulations. (The ethical and political importance of locating this or any problem at the level of discourse will be discussed further in chapters 4 and 5.)

As a constructionist project, queer theory is also concerned with language and the discursive effects of terms produced within the gender and sexual systems. Queer itself is not an identity constitution of its own; it is a resistance to the limiting strictures of so-called descriptive identity categories, including "queer." As we saw with Max and Kim, stable categories of male and female, and gay and straight, are discursively produced fictions within gender and sexual performances.

Another of the most significant discursive products of the binary systems is the "coming-out" narrative, critiques of which are central to queer theory. While a thorough discussion of this critique will be provided in chapter 4, social construction reveals that "coming out" is a declaration and embrace of a fixed and unified identity, an "authentic self."

HOW DID WE GET SO QUEER? A BRIEF QUEER HISTORY[4]

Sexuality, then, does have a history—though not a very long one.

—David Halperin, queer theorist

I wanted to participate in this project because it creates a history—I see myself as part of something.

—Courtney, Q-Squad member

Just as social construction is a philosophical position that emerged in response to the universalizing project of modernity, the notion of "queer" was born in response to specific discursive effects of the modernist project: the embrace of fixed gender and sexual identities and the assimilationist politics of the contemporary gay and lesbian rights movement (Crimp, 1993; Halperin, 1997; Jagose, 1996; Seidman, 1993; Warner, 1999). Critical to a situated understanding of this history is Foucault's (1978a) contention that homosexuality[5] as an identity is an invention of the modern era. While individuals across time and place have engaged in same-sex activities, classifying people based on those activities, thus rendering an identity category, had never before occurred. Foucault (1978a) dates the invention of homosexuality to an 1870 article by psychiatrist Carl Westphal. Foucault observes:

> We must not forget that the psychological, psychiatric, medical category of homosexuality was constituted from the moment it was characterized. . . . Homosexuality appeared as one of the forms of sexuality when it was transposed from the practice of sodomy onto a kind of interior androgyny, a hermaphrodism of the soul; the homosexual was now a species. (p. 43)

Here Foucault explicitly points to the productive and constitutive nature of discourse, as well as the social construction of an identity. Foucault also noted that this discourse, which started out as a disqualifying medical discourse, eventually was claimed and leveraged by homosexuals as a way to mobilize politically: "Homosexuality now began to speak in its own behalf to demand that its legitimacy or naturality be acknowledged, often in the same vocabulary, using the same categories by which it was medically disqualified" (p. 101). By employing this reverse discourse,[6] homosexuals became activists, setting their place at the societal table by "being" the very thing they were oppressed for.

This particular reverse discourse has been an example of history repeating itself. The homophile movement, which included organizations in the United States such as the Mattachine Society (an officially mixed-gender but overwhelmingly male group) and the Daughters of Bilitis (an exclusively female group), started with an agenda of social change rooted in a Marxist analysis of oppression. Over time, these groups developed a more cautious, assimilationist approach, which included disavowal of cruising, the sex trade, drag queens, butch dykes, and others who transgressed gender specifications (Katz, 1976). The primary message of the homophile movement shifted from a need to change society to a focus on homosexuals being just like everyone else—that is, heterosexuals.

Having lost its radical agenda and consequently its more radical membership, the homophile movement gave way to gay liberation. The 1969 Stonewall riots function as the iconic definitional moment of the gay liberation movement—a political effort that stood, again, for a radical agenda of social change. Stonewall did not happen in a vacuum; indeed, the United States in the 1960s and early 1970s was a crucible of progressive social movements, resistance to the authority of the dominant culture, sexual liberation (partly by virtue of the invention of the pill) and a substantive call for social justice and social change.

While it is easy to understand that Stonewall represents gay and lesbian resistance to heterosexist oppression, it is critical to queer understandings and politics to also understand what Stonewall meant to the resistance of the increasingly assimilationist position of the homophile movement. As these earlier movements became more normative, those gender and sexual outlaws who were pushed to the margins pushed back (Jagose, 1996). Among those usually placed at the epicenter of the riots are African Americans, Latinos, drag queens, and various gender transgressors.

Central to gay liberation was a prideful embrace of a gay identity. Shunning the embodied shame of the apologist homophile movement, which accepted the medical and psychiatric discourse of homosexuality as pathology, gay liberationists targeted the American Medical Association and the American Psychiatric Association (Alinder, 1992). Jagose (1996) notes that two factors, "the public assumption of gay identity and the discrediting of professional opinion," (p. 38) marked the difference between the liberationist and the homophile movements. Central to the liberationist strategy was the importance of "coming out" and the production of the coming-out narrative of an authentic, true self (Jagose, 1996).

This successful reverse discourse, resulting in the discursive creation of a stable gay identity, also resulted in the further marginalization of those not accounted for in the binary systems of gender and sexuality. Thus, history repeated itself: the gay liberation movement—conceived out of a radical response to the developing conservatism of the once-radical homophile movement—found itself trafficking more uptown than downtown.

Seidman (1993) describes the change in the gay and lesbian movement as moving from a liberationist to an ethnic model. That is, rather than seeking *legitimate* space for a constituency based on differences, the movement's efforts were focused on the establishment of a specific gay identity that was entitled to a *protected* space through the granting of civil rights. The civil rights/ethnic model, based on the notion of "equal but different" (Jagose, 1996, p. 61), required the establishment of a visibly identifiable gay and lesbian constituency in order to grant legitimacy. This process of legitimation of certain kinds of lesbians and gays—overwhelmingly white, middle class, able-bodied, monogamous, vanilla—meant the marginalization of others, many of whom had found a place in previous iterations of the movement.

Queer theory casts a critical eye on these results of the contemporary gay and lesbian rights movement and the ideologies that produced them. Cultural theorist Lisa Duggan (2002) coined the term *homonormativity* to describe this emergent gay cultural standard as "a politics that does not contest dominant heteronormative[7] assumptions and institutions but upholds and sustains them while promising the possibility of a demobilized gay constituency and a privatized, depoliticized gay culture anchored in domesticity and consumption" (p. 179). Thus, homonormative gays and lesbians, by abandoning the radicalized mission of the movement that inspired the Stonewall riots (e.g., challenging gender norms and promoting sex positivity), "have settled into a fairly bourgeoisie lifestyle—at the expense of those with less age, race, or class privileges, or those for whom this life does not fit" (Tilsen and Nylund, 2010).

Thus both the homophile and the gay liberation movements reflected the dominant patriarchal arrangement of American culture. Sharing same-sex desires did not make gay men and lesbians equal or equivalent within the gender system that privileges men and maintains an indifference to women's struggles for parity in income, employment opportunity, and personal safety. As a response to this dominance, lesbian feminism emerged. This movement emphasized that a one-size-fits-all political movement didn't offer women's sizes; indeed, assuming the umbrella term "gay" had the effect of invisiblizing women and reifying the centrality of men. Furthermore, lesbian feminists argued that organizing around gender was more important than doing so around sexuality. Lesbian feminists' struggles to have a place and a voice were not limited to the homophile and gay liberation movements, where they staged resistance to misogyny; they also challenged the homophobia that permeated the emerging women's liberation movement. (Betty Friedan [1963], a founding mother of women's liberation, infamously dubbed lesbian feminists—and their insistence on inclusion in the larger feminist project—"the lavender menace.")[8] The lesbian feminist critique of gay liberation and similar analyses from other nonhegemonic positions also criticized the movement for its assumption of a white subjectivity.

INTERSECTIONALITY AND BECOMING VISIBLE IN THE QUEER SPHERE

Queer cannot be discussed in terms of sexuality and gender alone, because it is not through sex and gender that we live our lives.

—Linda Garber, queer theorist

I had a boyfriend who was like, "You're brown—I like brown boys." And I'm like, "Great!" I don't see myself as brown. It was weird. It was fucking annoying when I found that out. It was like part of the pursuit of ME was because of my race. That's fucking offensive.

—Ruben, Q-Squad member

Representations of gay, lesbian, bisexual, and queer peoples have traditionally been white skinned in gay and lesbian studies and queer theory literature (Garber, 2003; Hammonds, 1997; Moraga & Anzaldua, 1983; Munoz, 1999; Quiroga, 2003). When organizing around the single identity of "gay" or "lesbian," sexual orientation effectively becomes the sole defining characteristic at the expense of other significant sites of identity production, especially race, ethnicity, and class. This reductionistic and totalizing view of identity attempts to make issues of race, ethnicity, and class inconsequential. The relegation of race to that of a footnote in most gay, lesbian, and queer histories and writing thus strengthened the dominant racial narrative and structures (Higgonbotham, cited in Hammonds, 1997).

Butler (1993) calls for a conceptualization of power that refuses to configure "racism, homophobia and misogyny as parallel or analogical relations" and considers the ways in which each of these forms of power "require and deploy each other for the purpose of their own articulation" (p. 18). Challenging the "bifurcation of race and sexuality" (Glick, 2003), some queer theorists of color argue for an intersectional approach (Crenshaw, 1993) as a way to negotiate individuals' multiplicity of identities. Without such an approach, the specifying and discourse-reifying regimes of normativity "keep subjects from accessing identities" (Munoz, 1999, p. 8).

An intersectional approach to identity requires that we acknowledge the complex relational and political realities of racially marked constituencies. This also requires a certain reliance on strategic essentialism. Cultural critics of color (Gopinath, 2005; hooks, 1994; Manalansan IV, 2003; Munoz, 1999) have argued that notions of a socially constructed identity can be easy to theorize and live by from a privileged racial and class position. From marginalized social locations, however, constructionism is viewed as a luxurious, primarily white enterprise that disallows group membership (i.e., the legitimacy of organizing around an identity category such as race or ethnicity). Furthermore, as Hammonds (1997) observes, race and sexuality are also gendered (and gender and sexuality are racialized). She points out that black feminists have repeatedly critiqued white feminists for failing to put forth a "conception of a racialized sexuality" (p. 137).

Spivak's strategic essentialism enables queers of color to operate from a position that neither fully rejects nor fully endorses social construction and queer theory assertions about identity. Instead of a unified gay and lesbian identity that privileges sexual orientation as the definitive organizing feature of all queer constituencies, there can be a more complex and contingent constitution that honors racial and ethnic meanings of identity and social justice demands.

Munoz (1999) works through the "white problem" of queer theory in a most effective fashion, through "disidentification," a concept compatible with both intersectionality and strategic essentialism. Disidentification is a way of complicating the homo/hetero binary, allowing queers of color to neither assimilate nor anti-assimilate within the dominant sexual binary. Munoz writes:

> Disidentification is meant to be descriptive of the survival strategies the minority subject practices in order to negotiate a phobic majoritarian public sphere that continuously elides or punishes the existence of subjects who do not conform to the phantasm of normative citizenship. (p. 4)

Disidentification challenges the modernist/constructionist binary of essentialized vs. constructed identity. Munoz asserts that the point where these two concepts of identity meet is a site of meaningful struggle that imbues racial minorities with agency to create an oppositional identity. The disidentificatory person becomes a hybrid—someone who occupies a collection of identities. Some of their identities are marginalized and some privileged. This depends on the context. These identities do not necessarily exist together in a single space at the same time.

Consider, for example, Vanay, a South Asian man from India living in the United States. To ask him to "come out" to his family when he knows full well the negative consequences to both his family and to himself imposes a particular identity politic and value system on them. Many white-skinned American lesbians and gay men (and their straight allies) may accuse such an individual of so-called "internalized homophobia." Yet, if he were to publicly declare a queer or gay identity he would be disowned by his family and cause them great humiliation. Why is it that we don't accuse him of "internalized ethniphobia"? This is essentially what Vanay experienced from his white American friends who encouraged him to come out and give his family the quintessential queer ultimatum: "I'm here; I'm queer; get used to it." Quite cognizant of the injustice of homophobia embedded within traditional Indian culture, Vanay did not see any personal or political value in coming out to his family. Such a move felt to him like "having to choose between being queer and being Indian." Coming out to his family would make it "virtually impossible to visit India" and would cause his parents great unnecessary distress.

Vanay found support from other queers of color who relied on an intersectional analysis and a disidentificatory approach. He maintained his position of not coming out to his family while embracing a queer identity within selective circles in the United States. Finally, in an act of disidentificatory social justice, Vanay—embracing his privileged position as a man of economic means—made a large philanthropic donation to an Indian agency that works with youth who have HIV.

Another productive aspect of disidentification is its ability to salvage components of discourses that are both useful and problematic. A disidentificatory person has the capacity to engage a particular discourse while considering its limitations, and reworking it to leverage its more productive aspects (such as Vanay's financial contribution to an HIV/AIDS organization in India).

Hence, Munoz's notion of disidentification can thus be used as a political strategy to rearticulate queer theory for queers of color. Rather than abandon queer theory in totality, queers of color can understand how the ideas of queer theory can be both helpful and hurtful. By reworking rather than discarding queer theory, queers of color can also appreciate the political importance of queer theory while concurrently striving to rearticulate the discourse surrounding it.

I could not not be queer.

—Ruben, Q-Squad member

As clinicians, in what ways are intersectionality, strategic essentialism, and disidentification important? To begin with, these theoretical positions invite new understandings of how people may manage the multiplicity of worlds they traffic in. Decentering the primacy of queer identity also honors and makes visible the relational and political realities of racialized identities. Additionally, we can support clients in accessing services, engaging in political action, and affiliating with personally meaningful cultural practices. By partnering with clients in the rejection of the essentialist/constructionist binary of identity constitution, we usher in multiple possibilities for negotiating various contingencies, political agendas, and material realities in ways that are safe, relevant, and meaningful for queer clients who occupy a multiplicity of social locations.

NOTES

1. While de Lauretis's quote is useful in illustrating the constructionist shift from an essentialist to a relational construction of identity, there is a double-edged sword in its reliance on essentialist terms such as "lesbian" and "woman."

2. I must acknowledge my (mis)appropriation of Sheila McNamee's (1996a) title, *Out of the Head and Into the Discourse*.

3. Cisgender is a term favored by many transgender activists to mark non-transgender identity. Cisgender people experience congruence between the sex they were assigned at birth and their own self-identification as male or female.

4. I am writing as a white-skinned American and the history I am reporting is one commonly embraced in North America. A multiplicity of histories of same-sex desire and subjectivities across cultures could be reported.

5. Once the homosexual was invented, the invention of the heterosexual as its contingency was necessary.

6. As a medium for the flow of power, discourse can be reversed by changing the direction of power without changing the foundational ideas on which the discourse relies. In this example, embracing an identity based on sexual partners and practices and developing a pedagogy of

liberation based on it, does not serve to overturn the discourse; rather, it seeks to change the meaning and value placed on it.

7. *Heteronormativity* is the institutionalized assumption that everyone is heterosexual, or should be, and that heterosexuality is inherently superior and preferable to any orientations outside of heterosexuality. The term was coined in 1991 by Michael Warner.

8. For a more thorough explication of lesbian feminism, see Abbott and Love (1973); Daly (1973); Lourde (1980); Rich (1986); and Smith (1977).

Chapter Four

Queer as Youth

Resisting the Homonormative of Identity Development

> *. . . one of the things that "queer" can refer to: the open mesh of possibilities, gaps, overlaps, dissonances and resonances, lapses and excesses of meaning when the constituent elements of anyone's gender, of anyone's sexuality aren't made (or can't be made) to signify monolithically.*
>
> —Eve Sedgwick, queer theorist

> *I think the most damaging part of labels is other people putting it on you and thinking they can understand you like that.*
>
> —Courtney, Q-Squad member

Gay-related content, gay imagery, and gay-identified people no longer carry the don't-ask-don't-tell patina in many areas of contemporary American society. As these very words are being written, another state moves closer toward legalizing gay marriage. The 2009 *American Idol* runner-up's hot and sexy gayness, not to mention his picture, were on the cover of *Rolling Stone*, Lady Gaga has everyone singing that they were "born this way," several Major League Baseball teams and other professional sports teams have produced an "It Gets Better" video,[1] and *Glee* introduced a transgender African American student during its third season. As a constituency, people who identify as gay, lesbian, bisexual, and (to a significantly lesser extent) transgender are at the epicenter of this shifting of cultural plates. In fits and starts, society is starting to see LGBT and queer people on their terms. Yet, the theories most available to us practitioners have failed to do so. They continue to rely on essentialist notions of identity embedded within modernist psychological discourses of development. As Langdridge (2008) points out, dominant models of development "present difficulties when working with . . .

queer [italics added] clients" (p. 23). This isn't for a lack of alternative conceptual frameworks; queer theory offers us many useful theoretical maps. While the queer theory literature offering these ideas is ample, it is primarily found in areas not likely to be accessed by most practitioners, such as anthropology, sociology, gender studies, cultural studies, literature, and other interdisciplinary bodies of scholarship (Langdridge, 2008). The purpose of this book is to bridge the gap between these ideas and practice.

Models of identity development are particularly germane to this discussion, as we have culturally and professionally coalesced around the notion (first introduced by Erickson some fifty-plus years ago) that developing a stable identity is young people's primary task. In this chapter I present queer theory as a relevant alternative to the prevailing models of development for those who work with queer youth.

STAGE ONE: RESISTING HEGEMONY

> *Society establishes the means of categorizing persons and the complement of attributes felt to be ordinary and natural for members of each of these categories.*
>
> —Erving Goffman, sociologist

> *I feel like sex is a big part of being queer but you don't lose your queer title because you're not having sex.*
>
> —Dylan, Q-Squad member

You'll recall from chapter 3 that Foucault (1978a) traced the invention of the homosexual to 1870. While people had been engaging in all kinds of sexual practices with partners of all genders across time, never before had a classification been articulated based on these practices. Foucault (1978a) notes that, while sodomy had been a criminal act, rendering the "perpetrator . . . nothing more than the juridical subject" (p. 43), the nineteenth century created the homosexual, who became "a personage, a past, a case history, and a childhood, in addition to being a type of life, a life form, and a morphology . . ." (p. 43).

Thus, an *identity,* and a concomitant specifying discourse, was constructed based solely on people's choice of sexual partners. This has fueled the argument that people are "born gay" (something that will be taken up in greater detail later in this section) and perpetuates binary notions of male/female and hetero/homo. Essentializing specifications (for example, blue for boys, pink for girls; men are rational, women emotional; females are born with vaginas and clitorises and males are born with testes and penises) are produced and maintained through language and discourse (Tilsen & Nylund, 2010).

As we have seen, through the reverse discourse that is the embodiment of the contemporary gay and lesbian rights movement, naturalized accounts of sexual and gender identity have been leveraged in the name of civil rights for many who claim LGBT identities. From a queer[2] perspective, however, this serves to reify essentialist specifications that regulate people whose lived experiences (or whose *preferred* lived experiences) fall outside the male/female, homo/hetero binaries, as well as for those who construct families and relationships in ways that challenge the dominant and validated constructions of these social institutions (e.g., bisexuals, genderqueers, individuals who are transgender or transsexual, relationships that are open, and people in polyamorous relationships).

Foucault (1978a) observes that claiming a fixed identity as homosexual, while perhaps personally liberating, unintentionally privileges heterosexuality. Cultural theorist Lisa Duggan's (2002) notion of *homonormativity* (discussed in chapter 3) describes this discursive effect as an assimilationist, normative, and privatized political agenda. In this way, homonormativity is exposed as a tactic of heteronormativity.

But what about the argument, to quote Lady Gaga, that, "I was born this way"? Where does that fit within the crossroads of queer theory and social construction? In deconstructing models of identity development, am I suggesting that people have a choice about their sexual identity? Doesn't the "born that way" explanation account for identity constitutions, while providing the strongest platform for civil rights?

First, a constructionist perspective rejects the "biology vs. construction" binary and assumes a "both/and" position. All knowledge is understood to be contextually contingent and mediated by culture, including material generated from "hard sciences" such as biology and genetics. However, social construction does not exist in binary opposition to hard science; indeed, hard science is an important frame, and social construction does not out-of-hand reject any particular discursive frame. Instead, it poses questions such as, *What are the effects of this discursive position?* and *What position(s) will be the most useful?* In practice, I would never challenge a client who understands him- or herself as having been "born this way." I would support this, while also being curious about how this discourse is useful. What does it afford those who use it?

Butler (2006) provides an excellent example of this approach to the gender identity disorder diagnosis (GID, a diagnostic category scheduled for removal from the DSM-V in 2013).[3] Noting that "for some the diagnosis seems to mean life, and for others, the diagnosis seems to mean death" (p. 276), Butler emphasizes the need to ask, *How is the diagnosis lived?* Where sexuality and desire are concerned, I would be interested in understanding how people *live* and embody a naturalized account of themselves and their sexual desires. How (and when and where) is this liberating? How (and when and where) is it limiting? Nothing goes unmediated (I would add, *especially* nothing about sex and sexuality given the hypersexualized commodification of sex in popular culture). We can, however, seek to understand how certain operations of discourse influence the meanings made in the production of identities. Furthermore, I make the critical distinction between "being born with" *desires* and "being born with" *an identity* that is a discursive production.

Thus, we again have both/and rather than an either/or. What is problematic about constituting a fixed identity—inherent or constructed—*based on desires*[4] is that specifications are created. That is why people who occupy the dominant center of sexual identity—those who meet the specifications of compulsory heterosexuality—don't have to make the claim of having been "born this way."

This claim can have both positive and negative effects for those embracing the naturalized account of sexual identity. As part of the reverse discourse that is the contemporary gay rights movement, it provides further traction toward organizing for legitimacy. It also leverages an important and influential prevailing discourse in modern society—empirical science. Science shows us that nature likes variation. It is we humans who try to limit choices, often demanding either/ors. (On the other hand, some religious and conservative positions have appropriated the idea of an "inferior biology" and used this as an argument against legitimizing a variety of sexual orientations.)

What about the idea that it's a choice? An old anthem, one that is still heard at times within the contemporary gay rights movement, is, "You get to love whoever you want to." While this would seem to be a sensible declaration to be made within a social system that privileges the rights of individuals, it has been appropriated by right-wing groups to legitimize so-called "conversion therapy." In this practice (condemned by all medical and counseling organizations including the AMA and APA), people are counseled into heterosexuality. This practice only makes sense if sexual desire is seen as a choice (which also suggests that heterosexuals are making a similar, albeit sanctioned, choice).[5] Thus, an important way to stage resistance to this harmful practice is to make the claim that people are "born this way."

Assuming a biological or genetic basis of sexual orientation not only erases the notion of choice, it also implies many LGBT people would, in fact, choose differently (that is, to be straight) if they could. Why, after all, would anyone *choose* to "be" something so reviled by society? Thus, being "born this way" is situated within the straightjacket of compulsory heterosexuality. The problem isn't that someone is naturally not heterosexual or cisgender; rather, the problem is compulsory heterosexuality and the gender binary. Furthermore, from a queer theory perspective, the problem is insistence on stable, immutable identity constitutions and homonormative specifications.

As a friend of mine says, "I was born this way not to believe I was born this way." Again, we have the both/and: ideas from essentialism and constructionism existing in a mutually influential manner.

From the constructionist perspective, another problem exists with the discourse of choice. This discourse implies full freedom or free will—a robust product of modernity, liberal humanism, and capitalism. To the constructionist, we are never totally free, since we live within the specifications of particular discursive constructions. Furthermore, many of those constructions leave us feeling that "choice" is not possible. Each discourse generates its own logic, and within that logic, there are moral, political, and ethical obligations. No discursive space offers completely free choice. Said another way, we can never completely rise above or beyond discourse; we can, however, deconstruct discourse and critique its effects in order to make new (and possibly transgressive or resistant) choices.

There are two more points I'd like to consider. I have said that social construction is interested in finding the most useful or meaningful discursive frame. This requires us to ask this question: *The best frame for whom, or for whose purposes?* As you can see, the various frames available—biological, construction, or choice—can all be deployed from different political positions with different agendas, and with different consequences for queer youth.

Which leads me to the last point to consider: In terms of securing civil rights, which position affords the greatest potential? Again, it is important to ask, *civil rights for whom, as determined by whom?*

For Reflection: Back to Practice

- *What are the practice implications of challenging naturalized accounts of identity?*
- *How have you typically understood sexual and gender identity? How have you thought of it for heterosexual and cisgender people?*
- *Think of some questions you may ask a client from each of these frames: (1) Sexual identity is natural or biological; (2) identity is a choice; and (3) identity is constructed.*
- *Write the story of your own sexual identity development from your preferred frame. What has influenced how you think of this story? If you had told this story five or ten years ago, would you have told it the same way?*

STAGE TWO: UNDOING DEVELOPMENT

The first thing that happened after I broke up with this guy was that I was out with a friend and two people came up and said, "So, are you guys dating?" And we're like, "NO!" and they said, "Well what are you?" And she said,

"I'm a dyke" and I said, "I'm a queer" and they're like, "What are you, what are you, what are you??" So, then I'm like, "Well, I don't think that's an appropriate question" because it was a question on their terms to help them feel comfortable, not a question to understand me on my terms.

—Sarah, Q-Squad member

Life histories are histories of becoming, and categories can sometimes act to freeze that process.

—Judith Butler, queer theorist

Sarah's lament about this multitude of assumptions offers a sage analysis of many cultural (and professional) assumptions that often inform how we interact with others. These assumptions gain power through their invisible ubiquitousness, a hallmark of a culture steeped in naturalized accounts of personhood and a dogmatic insistence that we all exist neatly within stock categories. Sarah was troubled that she had to defend and define her identity—and was pushed to do it on others' terms. Her resistance was perhaps equally unsettling for those who did the inquiring about her identity. With their compasses spinning, unable to grab onto the "true" north of essentialized identities, these young people dug harder into what *they* knew—prefabricated and reified identity classifications—rather than listen to Sarah on her own terms.

We operate in a discursive climate in which the question *"What are you?"* is considered viable and reasonable to pose to others. This is particularly the case—and particularly problematic—in therapy. After all, we have to know what kind of person we're working with, don't we?

For clinicians, the practice literature abounds with conceptual and practice guidelines for working with gay, lesbian, bisexual, and to a lesser degree, transgender youth,[6] including Savin-Williams's 2005 APA Distinguished Book Award–winning *The New Gay Teenager*. Much of the body of work (e.g., Bell & Pepper, 2008; D'Augelli & Patterson, 1994, 2001; Mallon, 2001, 2009; Morrow, 2004; Ryan & Futterman, 1998; Savin-Williams, 1990, 1998, 2001, 2005; Savin-Williams & Cohen, 1996) focuses on the identity development of LGBT youth—specifically, the emergence, acceptance, and integration of a gay, lesbian, bisexual, or transgender identity. This process, variously referred to as "identity formation" (Cass, 1979, 1984), "identity acquisition" (Troiden, 1979), "identity development" (Coleman, 1981–1982), and "differential developmental trajectories" (Savin-Williams, 1998; Savin-Williams & Diamond, 1997) are all informed to varying degrees by prevailing discourses of psychological development. Furthermore, all are inextricably and uncritically linked to—if not, indeed, *productive of*—the "coming-out" narrative.

From a queer theory perspective, the notion of identity "development" is problematic from the outset, as the implication is that there exists some essential, core constituent that in fact, *can develop*. Butler (1990a) challenges the assumption of a unified identity—homo- *or* heterosexual. This assumption effectively delimits unknown possible identities from emerging. Indeed, as Lesko (2000) notes, the developmental narrative created for queer youth is one for which adults know what the "correct" ending is. Also, Talburt (2004) points out that developmental models treat homosexual identity development as "natural" ("I was born this way") in order to avoid pathologizing sexual minorities. While understandable in their historical context and admirable in intentions, discourses that naturalize aspects of identity run the risk of prescribing identity more than describing it. Furthermore, these models treat youth as passive actors in a developmental design predrawn by adults (Lesko, 2000; Patton, 1996)—again a problematic assumption from a queer theory perspective.

Finally, even the more recent models created specifically for youth that attempt to account for contextual variables such as culture, class, race, etc. (e.g., Savin-Williams, 1998, 2005) continue to rely on modernist notions of a stable identity at the expense of understandings that allow for a proliferation of identity performances (Langdridge, 2008). While Savin-Williams (2005), for example, successfully demonstrates the need not to conflate identity with desire and sexual practice (he insists on using the identifier "same-sex attracted youth") he is adamant that all youth experience some manner of standard developmental process through which they become who they are. Furthermore, Savin-Williams summarily dismisses "queer," going as far as to claim that queer was a "flash" in the 1990s. Kuban and Grinnell (2008) write a smart and pithy critique of Savin-Williams's notion of the so-called "new gay teenager," observing that his celebration of assimilation is a "calling for the erasure of the multiplicity of queer identities" (p. 78). They are particularly pointed and poignant in their analysis of Savin-Williams's assumption that the "new gay teenager" occupies (and desires) a middle-class urban lifestyle. They suggest that for every youth that Savin-Williams claims to have found who recoils at the use of the word "queer" as a signifier, there may be countless queer-identified youth for whom Savin-Williams's model is too specifying, and, consequently, invalidating.

Any model of development, even one that claims that there is no monolithic way to develop and that each individual's course will look different (e.g., Savin-Williams, 2005), still carries with it two absent but implicit questions: *What does it mean for someone who* doesn't *"develop" in the way described by the model? Does this render some youth as developmentally disabled if they fail to develop in the prescribed ways?* Butler (1990a) notes that socially constructed norms gain status as "developmental law," thus ignoring that "the gendered body is *performative* [italics added]" (Butler, 1990a, p.173). For queer youth who see identity as something they *do* rather than something they *are*, adherence to notions of development can constitute a kind of spiritual violence, an experience of colonization into a way of being that does not fit with their own subjectivity or relational ethic. Consider, for example, Courtney's story of her experience with a therapist:

> *Courtney:* When I was dating someone that identified as trans . . . [the therapist] had a really big problem with that in relation to my identity, feeling like I was purposely seeking out someone who didn't have a solid identity because I was uncomfortable with creating a solid identity for myself, and, maybe she was right. But it felt more like she didn't understand where that person was coming from. She was using something that was real in my life to try to illustrate what she deemed as my problem.
>
> *Julie:* I'm wondering, what effects that had on you when she seemed to be promoting or insisting that the goal was a solid identity?
>
> *Courtney:* It was met with a lot of resistance a lot of the time and there was a lot of back-and-forth.
>
> *Julie:* You were trying to resist that?
>
> *Courtney:* Yeah! Maybe that's why I ended up feeling so crappy after therapy most of the time . . . there was that constant navigating, trying to come to concrete things that I thought I should do, and it just didn't fit.

A critique of developmental models may be read in Halberstam's (2005) notion of "queer temporality," which is, in part, a disruption of the youth/adult binary. This binary, Halberstam argues, is supported by "a life narrative divided by a clear break between youth and adulthood" (p. 153), a prevailing discourse implicitly produced and reified through notions of identity development. "Queer temporality" also refers to a general disturbance and challenging of conventional notions of time. Queer youth's disruption of developmental timelines is an act of resistance to normative specifications of time. Thus, queer temporality is a process of *queering time.*[7] Halberstam suggests that queer identity performances often include an extended period of youth. This challenges the notion of moving through a predictable or normative period of adolescent development toward a stable adult identity.

Queer theory reminds us that not only are various *models* of gay youth identity development informed by discourses that inhabit particular sites of cultural power and influence; the very construct of *development* itself is also produced and policed by those discourses.

Perhaps Butler and Byrne (2008) say it best: "Queer . . . cannot be easily accommodated in most psychological models" (p. 90).

For Reflection

- *What are your thoughts about Sarah's and Courtney's experiences?*
- *What do their experiences reveal about some of the ideas that inform therapists, both culturally and professionally?*
- *Imagine you are Courtney's therapist. She has just shared with you that she left therapy feeling crappy because she understood you to insist that there was a problem with nonstable identities. Think of your possible responses from each of the three frames: natural or biological; choice; and constructed.*
- *What would be the implications for you, both personally and in your practice, if you were to embrace the notion of "queer" as it pertains to fluid and flexible identities?*
- *Whom can you think of in your life (both personally and professionally) who has not followed traditional trajectories of identity development?*

STAGE THREE: COMING IN FROM COMING OUT

> *I don't think that queer has to do with sex. I think that queer has to do with being completely crazy.*
>
> —Ruben, Q-Squad member

> *. . . queer gets its political edge by defining itself against the normal rather than the heterosexual.*
>
> —Michael Warner, queer theorist

As we have seen, theories of identity development organize around, and are productive of, the "coming-out" narrative. Yet, compulsory coming out can be problematic for many people. In spite of this, the "coming-out" narrative often serves as the primary text guiding our work with clients. LGBT and straight therapists alike routinely coach their clients to "come out," lest they be found guilty of harboring "internalized homophobia," being "in denial" of their "true self," or even being dishonest. As a queer theory–informed therapist, I find this problematic on several counts.

To begin with, so-called internalized homophobia "perpetuates the injustice of privatizing socio-cultural problems, in this case, homophobia and heterosexism" (Tilsen & Nylund, 2010). Thus, individuals are wrongly cast as the problem when the problem lies in a culture that privileges the gender binary and heterosexuality, while pathologizing, criminalizing, denying civil rights to, and committing physical, sexual, and spiritual violence against people who fail to meet the specifications of the prevailing gender system.

For example, what cultural notions are we privileging when we uncritically encourage youth to "come out"? When we celebrate someone's "courage" for "coming out," isn't that an acknowledgment that there were risks involved? We cannot name and locate "courage" simply *within* an individual; the courage that person displays gains meaning because it occurs within a social context of risk, judgment, and hostility. I am not suggesting that we shouldn't acknowledge their courage; indeed, we thicken their story when we view it in context rather than as a naturalized quality. Yet, we may also understand another youth's refusal to "come out" as a practice of safety, caution, and good judgment—particularly given many young people's dependent status and/or economic and political disenfranchisement. Finally, for many queer-identified youth, not "coming out" can be a political statement, an act of resistance to notions of stable identity, and another way to underline the contextual nature of identity.

The modernist practice of dislocating individual narratives from the cultural narratives that create meaning and context perpetuates what Madigan (2008) calls the "burden of individualism." In the narrative therapy practice of externalization (White & Epston, 1990), which separates the person from the problem, problems are located in their cultural context. This creates discursive space for people to reflect on their relationship with these problems, as well as to protest the problems' effects on their lives. Thus, for example, we may ask a queer youth who chooses not to "come out":

- *What tells you that homophobia is still at large and that it's best for you to play it straight right now?*
- *Does coming out or being out have to be an all-or-nothing proposition? What are some options?*
- *Who else knows about and understands that your decision not to come out is to keep yourself safe?*
- *How would you describe the costs—what you sacrifice—in order to keep yourself physically safe?*
- *In what ways are you choosing not to come out in order to maintain important connections to other people, communities, or traditions that matter to you?*
- *What changes would you need to see to feel like things are safe enough for you to come out?*
- *Would you say that your very existence as a queer youth challenges heteronormative and homonormative assumptions?*
- *What would you say to someone who thinks you should just muster up the strength and "be honest" and come out?*
- *What's it like to feel pressured by other LGBT/queer youth to come out?*

These questions can open up conversational space that acknowledges the challenges of the social context for the youth. It also recasts "coming out" as an artifact of both the specifying gender and sexual system we live in and our culture of excessive individualism. The questions also honor the youth and their knowledge of the situation; acknowledge the dilemma of choosing physical and emotional safety at the expense of one's dignity and some relationships with others; acknowledge multiple complexities (both/and rather than either/or); and invite the imagining of possible futures.

Similarly, with youth who are in the process of "coming out," we can situate notions of "courage" and "honesty" within the contexts of heteronormativity, homonormativity, and homophobia. This avoids a common mistake made by therapists engaging in narrative therapy practices: externalizing only problems,[8] while essentializing so-called "positive" qualities, thus unwittingly reifying modernist notions of interiority. It also reduces poststructural and constructionist philosophies to a kind of linguistic gymnastics used only to isolate problems rather than as a worldview that stands in contrast to individualism. It also abandons the social-relational ethic central to the constructionist project and invokes capitalist metaphors of "ownership" and privatization (e.g., admonitions to "own" one's courage, honesty, strength, etc.). These qualities effectively become fixed within a self-contained individual, and they are no longer available as fluid, flexible resources—*the raw materials*—of identity. The productive enterprise that is identity construction and performativity, and the critical capacity to construct differing identities (or make different choices about coming out) for different contexts are thus abandoned.

What does this imply for practice? The critical implication is that we avoid a "thin" identity story (Geertz, 1973; Ryle, 1949; White & Epston, 1990) when we situate so-called "qualities" within the cultural contexts that give them meaning. When we externalize these resources for identity construction, we can richly develop the story of the "qualities" themselves, as well as the relationship youth have with them.

For example, in conversation with clients, they can explore and expand on the history and significance of these qualities; populate the story with other people who share knowledge of these qualities; and imagine a multiplicity of possible futures with these qualities. These generative conversations avoid the frequent dead ends of discussions positioned within the simplistic binary of vilifying problems and cheering on "strengths."

Another problem with these privatized accounts is their reliance on modernist notions of a "true" or "authentic" self. Requiring people to embrace their "true self" relies on essentialist constructions that ultimately lead to thin and rigid identity conclusions. They also imply the presence of a binary: true self/false self. Wilchins (2002) observes that binaries "don't give us much information" (p. 43), and the authentic/inauthentic discourse disqualifies those who construct and perform a multiplicity of identities.

Further, there is an implication that not to "come out" would be dishonest. Indeed, discourses of honesty are often invoked when well-meaning helpers encourage clients to "be honest about who you are." Foucault (1988) notes how these discourses lead individuals to engage in "truth games," a self-subjugating and regulatory practice that becomes difficult to distinguish from the policing and domination of others. Foucault considers therapy to be a practice that encourages both these technologies of the self and technologies of the domination of others.

From a queer theory perspective, what is in fact dishonest is the binary system that ignores the lived experiences of those outside it. Wilchins (2002) notes, "If the model and the body disagree, it is the body that must give way" (p. 41). When we insist our clients "come out" based on ideas of "honesty," we are maintaining cultural gender norms on the backs of our clients. "Coming out" can become another standard obligation of a homonormative culture, where policing from within the community is as strident as from without. Finally, "Coming out or being out is not an equal-opportunity endeavor" (Tilsen & Nylund, 2010, p. 98). People from various social locations remind us that issues of intersectionality must be considered in order to account for the differing consequences for coming out in different communities. Indeed, when working with youth, we must always attend to their lived experience *as youth*, and consider the ramifications of being out at school, at home, in their religious communities, and in all the environments they traffic in.

As we have seen, "coming out" exists within the terms of both heteronormativity and homonormativity; the politics of sameness; the psychology of authenticity; and the ascendancy of biological and genetic accounts of sexuality. These are all repeat performances of the developmental mantra, a mantra that leaves little room for variations on a theme.

When considering a queer youth's position on "coming out," it is important that we understand the youth's relationship to the idea of being "out" and to constructions of identity. Sadly, the policing of sexual identity is commonplace in our contemporary LGBT culture of homonormativity. This can take the form of charges that someone is "too gay" (e.g., not normative enough; perhaps a "flaming" man or butch woman; active in "militant gay agenda" politics) or that they are "not gay enough" (e.g., passing as straight; not "out" everywhere; not active in the "community"). Such policing and regulating occurs within the transgender community as well, as pressure exists to locate oneself as a transman or transwoman, rather than embrace a fluid position that transgresses the binary (Tilsen & Nylund, 2010). These specifying discourses can leave queer youth feeling oppressed from both outside and within LGBT subcultures.

So what do we do about issues of visibility, political voice, and access to services? How do we reconcile the tension between queer theory's rejection of identity claims and the lived reality of gays, lesbians, bisexuals, and transgender persons who see "coming out" as a necessary personal and political response to an oppressive sociopolitical climate? Halberstam's (2005) ideas are again useful here. Halberstam suggests that coming out and embracing a homosexual identity may be a *starting* point rather than an ending point. This very suggestion disrupts conventional notions of development. Indeed, most models of gay youth identity development mark various "coming-outs" (e.g., out to self, out to others, out to parents, etc.) as the final steps in integrating a unified and fixed identity. Yet, I have worked with many youth who transgress sexual and gender norms, and many are less invested in expert-produced categories than they are in fluid sexual vernaculars and the categories produced through local queer subcultures. Examples include genderqueers who embrace being "chicks with dicks," young women who identify as queer rather than lesbian, as a statement against essentializing second-wave feminist discourses, and transmen who desire other transmen and identify as "fags."

In acknowledging both the problematic and productive aspects of the "coming-out" discourse, the guiding question is not, *What is the "right" discourse?* No discourse is The Right Discourse. Rather, we may ask: *What discourse helps us construct an understanding that allows us to move forward in meaningful ways?*

Thus, while we may strategically embrace "coming out" as politically necessary, we can also work to resist the discursive limitations and the reification of norms that such a claim produces. This is the social justice potential of social construction and the liberatory possibilities of queer theory.

For example, I have frequently asked youth some variation of this question: *Who would you like to invite in as guests to your world, where you can be a respected host, rather than having to come out into a potentially hostile world as an unwelcome stranger?* When we turn the frame around, several discursive holds are released (Derrida, 1967):

First, the binary of in the closet/out of the closet is unhinged, and there is room for a contextualized performance of being "out." Second, the implicit value of "coming out" is challenged, and the universal privileging of "coming out" is revealed as a specification that leaves individuals little room for articulating their own ways of identifying. Third, it releases youth from the burden of individualism—from shouldering the responsibility for (and the potential risk of) moving through a hetero- and homonormative world. Instead, it allows them to exercise relational authority and responsibility for selecting safe-enough and appreciative people within specific contexts to participate in their lives. Fourth, it allows for a disidentificatory positioning for queers of color. Finally, it permits individuals to resist the sedimentation that can occur when claiming the fixed identity that "coming out" demands.

For Reflection

- *How have you thought about "coming out"?*

- *What position do you take with clients regarding "coming out"?*
- *What was new for you to consider in this section? What possibilities do you see? What is challenging for you?*
- *Do you think that straight people should practice routine coming out in solidarity with queers?*
- *Whom would you invite to come into your world if you wanted to create a meaningful and appreciative audience to your life?*

STAGE FOUR: THEORY AND PRAXIS—QUEERING THERAPY

> *This therapist was insisting that I am bisexual . . . or, that I've just not come out "fully" yet, whatever that means. I had to spend so much time trying to tell her, a) I'm queer, b) that's cool with me, and I'm as "fully out" as anyone can be, c) you should probably know something about this so you can quit telling your clients what the fuck they "are" and, d) that's not why I'm here anyway.*
>
> —Sarah, Q-Squad member

> *The judges of normality are everywhere. We are in the society of the teacher-judge, the doctor-judge, the educator-judge, the social worker-judge.*
>
> —Michel Foucault, philosopher and historian

As a practitioner committed to structuring safety and creating what Bird (2000) terms "safe enough" spaces for people to engage a proliferation of identities, I regularly challenge the discursive limitations and specifications of binary-based, essentialized accounts of identity, heteronormativity, and homonormativity. With youth, this means, in part, freeing myself from the prevailing developmental notions and "coming-out" prescriptions in order to make space for individual preferences and meaningful, unique outcomes. Queer theory provides a conceptual foundation for such a practice, one in which I can listen outside the box. Privileging the personal accounts of those I consult helps me avoid overtheorizing at the expense of people's lived experiences.

Rejection of essentialist notions of identity, and the developmental theories that support them, also shifts the gaze and dialogue of therapy from an intrapsychic, individual endeavor to the contextualized level of discourse. Individual identity narratives can then be considered in relationship to the larger cultural narratives that influence them. This helps illuminate issues of power and oppression produced and regulated through therapy practices born out of heteronormative and homonormative assumptions.

For example, on several occasions my clients have struggled against pressures that stipulate they must claim a fixed identity, "come out," or otherwise constitute their identity based on their sexual desires. In such situations, I shift the gaze to the discursive context that produces these pressures by asking questions such as:

- *What are some of the "rules" about "coming out" and being gay?*
- *Where do some of these "rules" come from—home, school, media, religion, other places?*
- *What do these "rules" say about the available categories that you have to fit into?*
- *What do the "straight police" say about these? The "gay police"?*
- *What might your own experience say about these categories and "rules"?*
- *Who would you like to have come into your world rather then you coming out to someone else's?*

By focusing on the specifying discourses of normativity, therapeutic conversations informed by queer theory can avoid identity constructions based on the idea of a natural or authentic sexual identity against which individuals can measure and justify (or fail to justify) their existence. These conversations can help reduce fears of being categorized and disciplined by normalizing gazes. Moreover, youth come to appreciate their own stand against normativity when their personal narrative is located within a politics of honorable resistance rather than pathologizing views of adolescent opposition, internalized homophobia, or developmental difficulties.

> *I came out as a lesbian first. Then I dated a guy. Telling my mom that I was dating a guy was horrendous. She's like, "You're a lesbian! What are you doing?" I said, "I like him, he's my friend; now we're dating it shouldn't be that complicated." You start questioning yourself. You thought you knew yourself. What is this? Am I a lesbian—is it I just like him? What do I do with myself? Where do I belong? Trying to grasp something so you can relate to anybody. That's why queer works for me.*
>
> —Mateo, Q-Squad member

Some queer youth performances of identity are not readily accounted for by the categories afforded us by language (e.g., gay, lesbian, bisexual, and transgender) (Tilsen & Nylund, 2010). "Queer" itself is often (and in this book) a critique of identities rather than a distinctive category of its own. This leaves us to wonder: Is it possible for us to capture in language identities that are fluid by definition, a "who you meet today may not be who you meet tomorrow" moving target? This is not an inconsequential matter of linguistic gymnastics, as labeling is a discursive practice that has significant bearing on how something is understood (Wilchins, 2004).

As therapists, then, what do we do?

Because our work depends on conversation and we exist in a language-based cultural economy, we can privilege queer youth knowledge and lived experiences over expert-produced models and delimiting specifications.

Consider Nick, an eighteen-year-old queer man I worked with. He cut his previously mid-back-length hair to just above his ears, a clean version of the hipster faux-hawk hairstyle. "Now," Nick said waggishly, "I just might have to be a boy for a while. I don't know. We'll see what the girls think of that." When I asked him what kind of boy he imagined being, he replied, "I guess that all depends on where I am and who shows interest. Who knows—maybe someone'll want me to be a tomboy. Could be fun."

Nick's attitude implied what Halberstam (1998) noted as "identity . . . as a process with multiple sites for becoming and being" (p. 21). These multiple sites are not only fluid and flexibile ("I just might have to be a boy for a while"), but they are also discursively produced and constituted in relationship (" . . . that all depends on where I am and who shows interest . . .). Cutting his hair as a cue for some potential "fun" also indicates the performative nature of these to-be-imagined, yet-to-be-constructed identities.

As for the person with the long hair left behind in the salon chair, what happened to that version of Nick? "Oh, he'll probably be back, in some shape or form, with or maybe without the hair. It's never quite the same, though. It's important to me to mix it up . . . keeps people on their toes, you know."

Nick's embodiment of performed sexual and gender identities—his ways of being that can be constructed, deconstructed, constituted, and reconstituted in a multiplicity of ways—are representative of what Butler (1990a) calls "a perpetual displacement . . . a fluiditiy of identities that suggests an openness to resignification and recontexualization" (p. 176) that effectively "denaturalizes" hegemonic meanings of gender and sexual identity. His lived experience of an embodied queer identity reveals both its constructed and performative nature—and stands outside the lines drawn by models of gay youth identity development.

To further advance a practice that challenges the fixity of language, Tilsen and Nylund (2010) offer these questions to help guide our work toward a more deliberate and productive use of language that is accountable to and respectful of queer constitutions:

- *How can we use language and discourse in ways that invite a proliferation of possible identity conclusions and performances, rather than discourses that mandate and regulate identities?*
- *What discursive positioning will allow queer youth's fluid and temporal identity performances (i.e., their lived experiences) to be seen as acts of resistance to stable, fixed, and binary identities?*
- *How can we structure safety and create discursive space that allows queer youth to bring all of themselves to therapy?*

- *How can we be responsible to engage in therapy practices that are in solidarity with queer youth's preferred ways of being?*
- *How can we position ourselves at the level of discourse in order to consider the effects of prevailing discourses on important people (e.g., parents, family members, other support figures) in the youth's life?* (p. 99)

These questions, and others like them, can help practitioners engage with clients in the deconstruction of internalized and decontextualized understandings that people may have about themselves. By assuming a position of radical doubt toward naturalized accounts of identity, we may enter into generative meaning-making conversations with queer youth that honor unique identity performances. Key to this positioning is allowing youth the discursive and relational space necessary to describe their preferred identities in their terms.

What answers can the Q-Squad provide to these questions? To begin with, they identified the need for therapists to use language that is inclusive, transparent, and open, and to attend to the power relations inherent in the therapeutic relationship. They also suggested that therapists avoid assumptions and reductive understandings, and that they embrace curiosity and humility. To paraphrase Courtney, we can never really know anyone: we can only keep working to understand them. In McNamee's (personal communication, May 20, 2011) terms, "Meaning is on the way."

Ultimately, this will allow us to be guided by questions rather than certainties, opening ourselves—and our clients—to unknown possibilities.

The potential consequences of such an investment during the therapy process proved to be a central point of conversation during one of the Q-Squad's inquiry meetings. Below is an excerpt from our conversation:

Dylan: Do you feel like you would have an easier time with a therapist who was part of the community?

Sarah: I feel like I would have an easier time with someone who used inclusive language. Regardless of whether or not they were actually queer.

Mateo: Yeah, as long as they were open and they shared that they didn't necessarily know what I was talking about, but they were willing to do the research and not expect me to explain it to them.

Sarah: Totally! Like that one therapist wanted me to educate her.

Mateo: You're the patient; that's not your job.

Sarah: Like saying something like, "I've never actually had a client that identifies as queer, but I'm going to do the best I can to understand where you're coming from, and if I don't understand then I'm going to do the best I can to figure it out."

Courtney: Isn't it just about asking questions, because when do we ever really know where someone's coming from just because they use a word?

Group: Yeah, yeah.

Sarah: I feel like it would be hilariously misguided to assume that because someone was part of the community, they would necessarily understand my experience as a queer-identified person. . . .

What can we do to learn from Sarah's experience and the insider knowledge shared by the Q-Squad? I keep in mind Wittgenstein's (1953) oft-quoted adage, *The limits of my language mean the limits of my world.* Yet what I have learned from my queer-identified clients suggests that turning this notion around—in effect queering Wittgenstein—is another way to challenge the truth claims of developmental models and resisting the fixity of identity categories. Thus, we could say, "My (queer) world exposes the limits of your (dominant and specifying) language" and the limiting categories offered within developmental models. Although the language of identity categories is limiting, and, indeed, oppressive, the existence of queer(ed) identities suggests that worlds are being created beyond the confines of the available language of identities.

STAGE QUEER: THE END IS NEVER NEAR—PROLIFERATING POSSIBILITIES AND RESISTING NORMATIVITIES

> *Queer is an umbrella term. You're sexual. There's no definition of whether you like guys or girls specifically. You are willing to work with what happens, whatever comes your way. You don't limit yourself.*
>
> —Dylan, Q-Squad member

> *What matters, I think, is how aware a person is of the options. How sad for a person to be missing out on some expressions of identity, just for not knowing there are options.*
>
> —Kate Bornstein, author and activist

Queer theory offers a conceptual framework that is consistent with the experiences of youth such as Nick and the members of the Q-Squad. Practice informed by queer theory can open up possibilities for queer youth for whom the notion of development proves specifying and rigid. Practitioners who are informed by queer theory, and the queerly constructed lived experiences of queer youth, can stand alongside their young clients in resistance to specifying discourses of hetero- and homonormativity.

IDENTITY, COMING OUT, AND JUSTICE: A CASE VIGNETTE

Ali is a twenty-one-year-old college student. She "came out" as a lesbian in her sophomore of high school. Recently, she has been moving toward a genderqueer identification. She sought therapy initially to help her with some decision making and anxiety around choosing a graduate school and all that would entail.

As those conversations progressed and she began to sort through the myriad decisions before her, Ali wanted to discuss how her new understandings of gender and identity were important in her life. These were pertinent to some of the decisions she would make down the road. Ali wanted to "have a better handle on where I'm headed with how I'm thinking about gender," because she felt that would help her make the best choices for her future academic and professional career.

In this first excerpt, Ali, recalls how she "researched and prepared" to "come out" in high school. I asked her about this, curious as to what she might want to carry forward from that process, and what she might consider doing differently in the future.

> *Ali:* I started reading everything I could find to learn what it meant to be a lesbian. I wasn't identifying yet, but I wanted to know. And I had started flirting and kissing other girls and stuff. If I was going to be this person, what was it that lesbians are like? What do they do? Do they gather in certain places? I didn't know.
>
> *Julie:* You were looking for the club handbook and decoder ring?
>
> *Ali:* Yeah! And I didn't like what I was finding. The Michigan women's festival, women drumming topless. I remember thinking, "If this is what it means to be a lesbian then I don't want to be one. Can't I just like girls?" I didn't find much written that seemed to be about me or people my age back then.
>
> *Julie:* Was it like you couldn't fit yourself into certain boxes, like how you're supposed to be?
>
> *Ali:* Yes. Boxes is exactly right. Boxes with rules.

Julie: As you read and researched, how did things start making sense for you? How did you find your way?

Ali: At some point, they opened up so it was more than the boxes. As I read more, I gained understanding that there are lots of ways to be gay and I was meeting more kids from other schools. And, I found out you don't have to play the drums to be a lesbian!

Julie: I play the drums! So, you were finding lots of different ways and meeting people. I'm wondering if there was a particular thing you read or someone you talked to or something that threw a light on a variety of ways of being that made you feel like you had a space and didn't have to fit into someone else's box?

Ali: My friends Sarah and Jennifer. They don't fit the boxes of what people typically think lesbians are. They were seniors when I was in tenth grade. We're all still friends. They stopped dating after high school but they stayed friends with each other. They're both very feminine and when they were out together nobody thought they were together . . . until some PDAs! And they identify more as queer now.

Julie: People didn't read them as a couple or as queer?

Ali: No—if you judge them by typical straight/gay stereotypes they look completely het.

Julie: And they've taken on queer more? How has that influenced you?

Ali: It helped eliminate the boxes. So, back in high school, it helped me be okay coming out as a lesbian knowing different kinds of lesbians. Now, they are people that I look to as I think about being more queer. But, they've had problems with other lesbians who don't accept them because they "look straight"—whatever that means! It's crazy. Who gets to say what's what? It's back to the rulebook. I don't like it.

Ali's account reminds us that heteronormativity erases the possibility that women who look like her friends might not be straight. Heterosexuality is assumed and standards of femininity are thought to separate straight feminine women from lesbian masculine women. Homonormativity creates specifications that exclude her friends because they don't seem "gay enough"—they can pass *too* well as straight. She explained that, as a high school senior, she ended up cutting her hair because she was "sick of boys hitting on me and being excluded by the other gay kids."

Julie: Was that a loss for you, to cut your hair, to concede perhaps to specifications?

Ali: At first I was pissed, and my parents were kind of freaked out about it. When I came out to them later, they were like, "Oh, the hair. That makes sense now!" I missed my hair and it took a while to get used to shorter hair. But it was liberating after just a few weeks. I was okay with people thinking I was a lesbian—I wanted it. That's essentially how I came out. Some friends thought I was doing it for the wrong reasons.

Julie: What would those be?

Ali: To fit in, for other people.

Julie: Is that how you experienced the liberation of cutting your hair?

Ali: No!

Julie: Did Jennifer and Sarah think it was for the wrong reasons?

Ali: No, they supported me doing what felt important to me.

Julie: What did it mean for you? What was important about it?

Ali: Well, I was pissed about guys asking me out and I thought, "If this is what is takes to get other girls to notice me, I'll do it." But I was at a place where I wanted to have people question, to wonder, to just not be able to peg me for sure.

Julie: Was that from Sarah and Jen's ideas about queer influencing you?

Ali: Yeah, totally. I mean, back then, they weren't talking or thinking about it that way quite yet, but it had that effect for sure. I wanted people to look at me and think, "I wonder . . ." Because in a way I wanted to wonder, too. Wonder about who I could be.

Julie: What was it about wondering—yours and others'—that appealed to you? What possibilities emerged, or things that you learned about yourself, about who you could be?

Ali: I didn't want other people to be so comfortable and sure about me without going through me. I realized I had some power in the way I could present myself. Not how people perceive me, I can't control that. But in different situations I have the power to choose what I look like. I have short hair—whatever that means—but I can wear super-girly clothes or what I find in the guy's department, but I have the choice.

Julie: What was doing the deciding for you before you realized you had a choice?

Ali: I guess you'd say society was. What a girl or boy is supposed to look like. What it looks like to be straight or gay.

Julie: Ali, as we look back to that time in high school when you were coming out, what signs of the queering that you are doing now can you see back then?

Ali: Huh, yeah. I hadn't thought about that, but I started out in some ways queering some stereotypes. I did cut my hair. But I'd wear skirts sometimes with Docs. And I never judged Jen and Sarah or others for not conforming to the gay patrol. I guess my whole thing with wanting to see what could happen is pretty queer, huh?

Julie: How has that experience—the research, coming out as lesbian, being out, and now moving into queer—prepared you for how you want to engage with gender now?

Ali: I guess it gets me thinking that coming out itself isn't like this thing. It's more like *I come into* what fits for me and the ideas and people that matter to me, how I want to be in the world. It's almost like, if I come out, people may have certain ideas that don't fit for me. I have to be clear about what coming out means and what it doesn't so I can continue to define myself.

In our next meeting, Ali continued to talk about gender and how she wondered whether she needed to come out as genderqueer. We talked a bit about the idea of performativity and gender and identity. We explored the usefulness and the limitations of coming out, how coming out as queer is the same or different process as coming out as lesbian, and how it is or isn't possible to stay fluid after coming out. Ali had read about some of those ideas and she agreed that she thinks gender is a performance. She talked about her "girl-boy struggle"—what she used to go through every day to decide what she wanted to wear and who she wanted the world to think she was.

Julie: What made it a struggle?

Ali: Trying to think about what others would think and psych them out. But I can't ever be sure what others will think. Now I make decisions just based on what I want. And of course, it does matter if I'm going to work or going to the gym.

Julie: What helped you move from the boy-girl struggle to where you are now?

Ali: I had to understand where my ideas about gender were coming from and understand that I don't need to have these strict gender guidelines in my life.

Julie: If you hadn't come to understand ideas about gender so that you could resist the strict guidelines, how would your life be different now?

Ali: I think I would just be following the rest of the fish in the stream.

Julie: Which fish?

Ali: Well, I don't think it would be straight fish because I really like girls a lot. But I could see continuing to struggle with how to be the right amount of gay, the right kind of lesbian. Fortunately, things have changed and there are more queer ways that are happening. But I think I got to them more quickly and with less compromise because I worked on understanding gender.

In our next meeting, Ali said that she had been thinking about coming out in terms of "personal safety versus social justice." She was struggling to reconcile the reality that there are times and places where being out as queer is not safe with the idea that not being out perpetuates the injustice of heteronormativity and homonormativity. We discussed how she makes those decisions and considered the importance of context and relationships in an effort to unhinge the all-or-nothing binary of out/not out. Ali found it very helpful to "remember to forget the all or nothing," noting that queer should be useful toward that end, as it promotes fluidity. She also acknowledged the pain of sometimes feeling forced to choose safety over "being herself." We situated this dilemma within the unjust binary systems that created this false choice.

I was curious about Ali's commitment to social justice and how that was a part of her coming-out process. She connected her interest in justice to the knowledge she had gained by examining how discourses about gender work.

Julie: Are there ever times you'd want to unlearn what you know about gender and go back to not knowing?

Ali: Sometimes when I'm with certain family members, yeah. But then I remember that they haven't been exposed to these ideas and that gender affects them, too. And sometimes when I'm around "really gay gay people," people that aren't into queer, lots of times they're older, and they don't think about race or trans stuff or other things that I think are really important.

Julie: What keeps you from going back to not knowing, pretending that you don't know?

Ali: I wouldn't want to. Why would I want to not understand how these things work? Or not want kids coming up to be ok with gender and sexuality? It's important because there are other people who don't fit in those boxes I worked to avoid. They need to know they're not alone. And that they're not the problem.

Julie: When you first came out and then started moving more toward queer, did you intend to take up for others, making this a project of social justice?

Ali: No, not at first. It was when I started realizing the opportunity I had to change people's perceptions about what women look like and what men look like and that there are more than just those two options.

Julie: Do you have a vision or a hope as to what a more just context for coming out might become for queer youth in the future?

Ali: I haven't really thought about that but, yeah. It's like everyone or no one comes out. Straight kids, too. Because, everything can be okay or a possibility for everyone, so you either tell people how you identify, or no one does and it doesn't matter. And it doesn't mean that everyone is like, pansexual and genderqueer—people like different things or are attracted to some genders and not others. It's just that it would be okay.

Julie: That's quite a vision of inclusion and justice. Five years ago when you were figuring out that you didn't want to drum topless, would you have ever thought up something like that?

Ali: Ha! Doubtful. But I'm not sixteen trying to figure out how to come out anymore. Now, I'm coming into all kinds of things!

Ali's story serves as a fitting example of the idea that coming out isn't an endpoint. Her reworking of coming out to "coming into" reflects the ingenuity of many queer youth, an inventiveness and flair available when specifications are questioned and binaries are exploded.

Through her relationships with Jennifer, Sarah, and others, Ali found some of the resources for constructing an identity that suited her. These resources also laid the path for her informed resistance to normativity—not only for herself, but also for others who needed allies.

REFLECTIONS ON CHAPTER 4

BY SARAH DACK AND COURTNEY SLOBOGIAN

While reading your ideas about the difference between identity development versus identity construction, we started thinking about how the concept of "queer identity development" suggests that it is an unfolding of an identity already constituted or "in place," as opposed to the idea of an identity constructed either consciously or as a result of social interaction. It seems like an important distinction, given that it again restores agency to youth and acknowledges the ways that identity is constructed.

This idea may work to eradicate any ageist assumptions and interactions that shape the power balance between care providers and youth. The switch from an understanding of "identity development" to identity construction actively debunks the potential for assumptions about the trajectory of a youth's "queer lifestyle" or "queer timeline." One such assumption includes care providers' belief that youth should "come out" or "be out to their friends" or label themselves. Another example would be making assumptions about a youth's personal identification based on who that youth is interested in sexually. This highlights the way that mainstream notions about identity development are sort of formulaic and exist in a way that means people can fail or succeed. For example, popular assumptions about development may include "a woman interested in women = lesbian; a woman interested in women and men = bisexual" without any exceptions. These assumptions intercept the care provider's ability to be truly supportive of someone's process of identity construction.

Basically, we're super impressed with this distinction between identity development and identity construction as an alternative mode of understanding queer youth experiences and the way this distinction can be potentially important to care providers.

NOTES

1. "It Gets Better" is a YouTube video project created by author Dan Savage in 2010. The project, established in response to the violence and harassment experienced by LGBT youth, features videos of everyday people, Hollywood stars, US senators, and even President Obama, all delivering messages of support and encouragement to youth experiencing harassment.

2. As a reminder, the term "queer" serves as a critique of identities, rather than as an identity constitution of its own, and is claimed by many youth in resistance to fixed identity categories. It is not meant to be an umbrella term for LGBT, although authors, especially those from noncritical disciplines, use it this way. Here, it is a signifier that stands against "normal"; it is taken up by some individuals who are gender normative and/or who have opposite-sex desires but for whom "queer" signifies their resistance to other regimes of normativity (see, for example, Thomas's [2000] *Straight with a Twist*).

3. I prefer to call GID *gender inflexibility disorder*. This is a diagnosis of the discourse, emphasizing the social location of the problem. Diagnosing discourses will be discussed in chapter 7. It will be interesting to see how the removal of GID from the DSM influences discourses of diagnosis and gender.

4. Of course, constituting a fixed identity based on *any* particular dimension of human experience creates specifications—what's okay and not okay—within that dimension.

5. Common anti-gay rhetoric features the argument that children will come to see the "gay lifestyle" as acceptable and will possibly choose it for themselves (after some serious recruitment by the sinners themselves).

6. Terminology in much of the current literature on LGBT youth development reflects a certain theoretical conflation. Often, "queer" is used as an umbrella term for the constantly morphing acronym, LGBT, inserting it where the authors mean "gay" but are striving for inclusivity. This divorces "queer" from its politics, fails to recognize its deployment as a critique of identity categories, and invisibilizes the multiplicity of identities it signifies. Also, it ignores the large body of queer theory scholarship generated in interdisciplinary fields.

7. Time is socially constructed. It does not hold the same meaning in all cultural locations or at (ironically) all points in history. For example, to "be on time" in some cultures might constitute being "late" in other cultures. Or, the idea of "passing" or "spending" time is not something understood in all cultures. Also, childhood and adolescence, concepts defined to a large extent by a measurement of time, are recent productions of the industrial age (Gell, 2001).

8. This practice is likely due, in part, to narrative therapy's focus on separating the person from the problem and its concomitant mantra, "The person is not the problem; the problem is the problem," as well as to a more general push toward so-called "strengths-based" practices.

Chapter Five

Bringing Sexy Back

Sex Positivity and the Rejection of Erotophobia

I think the most important thing that queerness has helped me with in terms of pleasure and desirability is recognizing that if I find someone attractive who has a body similar to mine it forces me to recognize that I'm okay. That's one of the most amazing things that desire and queer sex has shown me about myself.

—Sarah, Q-Squad member

People will only have the freedom to get their freak on, without judgments, when we find a way to get rid of the "freak."

—Jennifer Peper, gender and sexuality blogger

TWO GIRLS DOING IT: WHAT MY TEN-YEAR-OLD NIECE ALWAYS KNEW

Several years ago my partner Lauri and I were at home, waiting for my brother and ten-year-old niece to deliver our annual supply of Girl Scout Thin Mint cookies. We wanted those cookies. And, we were looking forward to a visit with my brother and niece, who affectionately referred to Lauri as "Bug" and to me as "Alien." We were her favorites and our whole extended family knew it.

My brother pulled up his truck in front of our house. But after several minutes, there was no knock. No doorbell. No ten-year-old blasting through our door with my Thin Mint order.

We looked outside and saw the two of them sitting in the truck. They sat and we watched from inside. For twenty minutes they sat and we watched.

Finally, my brother came to the door with the cookies but without his daughter. As we let him in, we saw the frustration, sadness, and helplessness on his face.

"She was so looking forward to seeing you guys and then we pulled up and she said, 'They have a rainbow flag! Ewww! I'm not going in there!'" The flag had always flown from our front stoop and this was not her first time coming over to our rainbowed house.

My brother said, "So, I asked her, 'Well, what do you think that means?' and she says, 'They're lesbians!' And I asked her, 'Well, what does that mean?' And she said, 'Two girls doing it!'"

As we have seen, the contemporary gay rights movement has relied on essentialist notions of identity, coupled with the apologist position of homonormative politics. Together, these have largely sucked the sex out of its quest for equal rights. Queer theorist Michael Warner (1999) has called the movement a "PG gay movement" (p. 42), accusing it of being founded on erotophobia. Warner asserts that at the core of queer ethics and culture is "dignity in shame." Warner calls for a political movement that goes beyond the parameters of sex or the identity politics of sexuality, a movement that recognizes that homophobia effects people other than gays (e.g., people whose gender performances stand outside the gender binary). This movement would recognize that being heterosexual is not protection for people who transgress—even a little—gender specifications or the highly delimiting code of morally approved sex practices. This is the same ethic that inspired the Stonewall riots.

Sexual freedom, economic justice, and the liberation of pleasure have historically been at the center of gay and lesbian politics. In the contemporary gay rights movement, however, these foci and their historical significance have been abandoned for a neoliberal gay rights agenda that privileges consumer rights over human rights and fosters economic and political mobility (Chasin, 2000; Duggan, 2002). Sex-positive and queer critics contest this philosophy and its historical amnesia, asserting that capitalism sabotages the potential for the kind of radical social change originally connected to identity-based movements (Chasin, 2000).[1]

De Vries (2008), writing as a self-identified "femme dyke as nelly fag" youth (p. 142), provides an insightful insider's critique of the effect homonormativity has on youth and sex education provided in American schools:

> I despise the way the mainstream gay movement has ignored the issues surrounding sex education in the United States. In-school activism, when spearheaded by gay adults, does not reflect the needs of queer youth, and often

> sidesteps the issue of sex education altogether (not to mention issues of age and ageism, dis/ability, race, class, and sexualities and genders that aren't strictly "male" or "female" and "straight" and "gay") . . . creating a safe school environment also means creating curricula that are inclusive of queer issues, including . . . sex ed curricula. (pp. 144–145)

De Vries insists that queer activism should reform sex education and "not just insinuate ourselves into already sorely lacking" curricula (p. 146). De Vries describes and applauds the safer-sex workshops she attended at queer youth centers and conferences, noting that traditional sex education is founded on abstinence and the view that sex is a "risk factor" to be averted, while the safer-sex education "took for granted that youth were interested in, and perhaps having, sex" (p. 143).

It is also critical to challenge the naturalization of the construction of "sex." As we have seen, Foucault (1978a) challenges the idea that sexuality is an immutable, "natural" quality of human beings; rather, it is culturally and historically contingent, produced through language and discourse. Foucault asserts that the Victorian age was not defined by the sexual repression (lifted partly by the sexual revolution of the twentieth century) typically associated with it. Indeed, because he rejects the very notion of the essentialized quality, "sexuality," there is nothing that can be repressed, and then liberated at a later time. Instead, Foucault maintains that sexual *discourse*, dynamically influenced by time and place, incites changes in human behavior, meaning, and experience. More specifically, Lenore Tiefer (2004) notes that what contemporary Americans recognize and mark as sexuality "would be quite unrecognizable to people living in different civilizations" (p. 17). For example, Foucault (1985) demonstrates the contingency of the contemporary identity markers of "homosexuality" and "bisexuality" as they impose modern Western meanings on other meanings local to particular places and times.

In short, sexuality (a capacity for sexual desire and expression, as opposed to identity—i.e., "sexual orientation") is *of* sex, but is not sex. We can extrapolate from this constructionist/Foucauldian analysis that "sex"—that is, particular sex acts—are also constitutive and contingent as well. I am not the first to ask how an Oxford- and Yale-educated Rhodes Scholar could claim that he did not have sex with an intern who gave him a blow job. That this claim was even available to him was due in part to the constructed nature of what constitutes sex. (The meaning is in the context of the aroused, perhaps?)

A queer re-visioning of sexuality rejects the modernist notion of a universalized "inner drive" in favor of a constructionist view of sexuality that is constituted in relationship, dialogically negotiated among people, and performative in nature. Further, it opens up the possibility that sexuality, as something produced through discourse, can resist specifications and regulating regimes, and be constructed in ways that are liberating rather than controlling.

Warner (1999) notes that acts of resistance to sexual regulations change in response to cultural shifts. He cites as examples the women's and the gay rights movements as liberatory projects that emerged out of different needs at different times. Furthermore, historical and anthropological inquires into sexuality (e.g., Ortner & Whitehead, 1981; Padgug, 1979; Weeks, 1981) since the constructionist turn have exposed the unstable and contingent quality of language and meaning, as well as the ever-shifting attitudes that define a cultural moment (Tiefer, 2004).

To *not* address sex and sexual justice, then, would result in several crimes against queer. Within a culture that breeds sexual shame, whose sexual curiosity is motivated by erotophobia rather than a celebration of pleasure (Warner, 1999), and which continues to legislate sexual morality, constructing a queer identity very much involves sex. However, this is (or at least can be) a sex founded on justice, inclusivity, and shared meaning, rather than sex shrouded in stigma and shame, and embedded in moralism. Claiming a queer identity informed by a queer political ethic is in part defined by taking a position on sex and sexual justice, creating an ethic that resists the prevailing cultural interdiction against the pleasures sex affords.

TEACH THE CHILDREN WELL

> Mateo: *It was so science-y—like* Star Wars*—watching the sperm going into the egg.*
> Julie: *Did it make you want to do it?*
> Q-Squad: *Nooooooo!!!!!*

A search for "adolescent sex/sexuality," "teen sex," "gay youth sex," "queer youth sex," "psychotherapy/counseling, youth, sex," and related terms exposes the dominating discourse that informs how we think and work with all youth around sexual matters. The overwhelming majority of search results are about "risk" factors, pregnancy, and sexual offenses. These results reflect the cultural proscription against nonmedicalized, nonpathologizing, and sex-positive conversations about youth sexuality. They also point to the dearth of practical and sex-affirming material available to help clinicians assist queer youth in matters relating to sex.

Review of practice-based literature focused on clinical work with queer youth exposes the crucible of identity politics, homonormativity, and erotophobia, where sex is seen as a risk to be "managed." Practice-based texts take great pains to ensure that the hallmark of contemporary gay identity politics—the separation of sexual identity from sexual activities—is clear. For example, in *Nurturing Queer Youth: Family Therapy Transformed*, Fish and Harvey (2005) lament that because "sexual identity and sexual practice are falsely merged, identity is rarely explored in family therapy practice" (p. 25). By taking up the discourse of "sexual identity" while disembodying it from erotic sexual practice, these clinicians reify erotophobic homonormativity and encourage the desexualization of queer youth.

While this tactic may make queer youth safer and more accepted (acceptable?) through the process of "normalization," it does so without addressing the lack of social and sexual justice that engenders such a maneuver. Where the authors do take up sexual practice, it is limited in discussion to inquiries about the gender of sexual partners. Nowhere is there a discussion of pleasure or eroticism, much less an affirmation of the nitty-gritty of sex.

The index of the award-winning *Lesbian and Gay Youth: Care and Counseling* (Ryan & Futterman, 1998) is revealing as well. After reading the several pages on "sexual abuse and assault," I encounter entries for "sexual history" (a bio-psycho-social risk assessment); "sexual intercourse" (subentries that follow: "early and unprotected; as HIV transmission route; postponing"; and "sexually transmitted diseases" [multiple subentries]). There is an entry for "sexual readiness assessment," a half page of text coaching practitioners on how to counsel gay and lesbian youth to "postpone sexual activity" (p. 84). There is no mention of pleasure or eroticism.

"You have no idea what a radical idea you are proposing, to incorporate talk of pleasure into sex education for youth," states Emily Scribner-O'Pray, a sexual health and youth work professional with over twenty years of experience (personal communication, October 11, 2009). Scribner-O'Pray agrees that educational, medical, and psychotherapy literature about queer youth sexuality in the United States focuses entirely on sex as a risk factor.

"Pleasure and eroticism are strictly off—capital 'O'—limits—capital 'L'—when doing sex ed," Scribner-O'Pray notes. "We are very scared of the idea of pleasure." In individual meetings with young people she refers them to a book about sexual pleasure "if they ask a specific question and are already sexually active. I would never hold the book up in a class and say, 'This is good—check it out!'" Scribner-O'Pray agrees that clinicians who are interested in taking up a more sex-affirming position with queer youth have to look outside their professional literature.[2]

In sum, where young people are concerned, sex is either framed as a moral public health issue or avoided entirely in the bulk of professional literature. Indeed, Rubin (1984) observes that "sex is presumed guilty until proven innocent" and, as Levine (2002) notes, this is even more the case when sex involves youth.

Perel (2006) notes that it is a particularly American position to view sex as "deeply dangerous" (p. 92) to young people. She contrasts this to the European perspective that sex is normal and healthy—a point that Scribner-

O'Pray also highlighted during our interview. Evoking a queer ethos, Perel states that the European tradition holds that "sex is not a problem; being irresponsible about sex is" (p. 92).

Thus, queer youth—doubly marked as "queer" and "youth"—have two prevailing discourses to contend with where the construction of identity meets sex and sexuality: homonormativity and erotophobia.

> *In my lesbian experiences of sex, it was given and taken like this commodity almost, this thing that could be given and taken. Like, I'm having sex with you but I might like her and I might take it away from you and give it to her. Like this moveable thing that isn't shared all the time. I think that queer makes it possible to start breaking that open.*
>
> —Courtney, Q-Squad member

SHAMELESS JUSTICE FOR ALL: FROM SEX NEGATIVITY TO SEX POSITIVITY

Warner (1999) explores the sexual shame that accompanies the reverse discourse of the contemporary gay rights movement. He maintains that gay culture is marked by shame (one need look no further than the ubiquitousness of the word *pride*) and observes that, in this culture, desires are legitimated (i.e., free from shame) only when proven to be "immutable, natural, and innate" (p. 9).

This embrace of an essential gay identity and its reverse discourse allowed gay activists to traffic in the moral economy of the culture by putting distance between their now naturalized (and, thus, normalized) homosexual identity and the sexual behaviors previously deemed morally reprehensible. The prevailing moralistic discourses produce the belief that sex is only acceptable if it is "unlearned, prereflective, present before history, and isolated from the public circulation of culture" (Warner, 1999, p. 9). In short, sex is made out to be a natural act: how you "do it" is because of who you "are." Gays and lesbians have found more and more seats at the sociopolitical table because more and more people accept this "fact" (bisexuals, however, often are forced to sit at the kids' table for their challenge to the immutability clause). To be thought of as just like everyone else (i.e., heterosexuals) has meant going sexually unmarked—just as heterosexuals do.

From a queer perspective, this delimiting naturalization of sex is problematic. To begin with, sorting out the immutable from the mutable aspects of desire and sex always serves a particular moral and political agenda. This has resulted in acceptance and legal protection for some forms of desire and not others. Although homosexual identities have gained cultural cachet, *this victory has happened on the backs of those whose desires and practices sit outside the margins of sexual normativity*, whether they identify as straight, gay, queer, or otherwise. This has created a list of victimless crimes that consenting people can, and routinely do, commit. Gaining "liberation" at the expense of those furthest from the societal center—and, indeed, contributing to the production and construction of that center—is no liberation.

In "Thinking Sex: Notes for a Radical Theory of the Politics of Sexuality," Rubin (1984) identifies a "sexual hierarchy" that privileges marital, reproductive, heterosexual sex and that pathologizes other sexual practices as abnormal, inferior, shameful. She also notes that there is a special stigma surrounding masturbation that, despite the increase of sexual health education campaigns, persists. This special seat of shame is worth noting for those that work with queer youth; masturbation is often the first, if not temporarily the only, available sexual practice for young people. Unearned privilege is conferred about those engaged in practices that fall within "the charmed circle." The charmed circle embraces "good, normal, natural, blessed sexuality" (p. 281) and includes practices such as:

- Heterosexual sex
- Performed within marriage
- Monogamous
- Procreative
- Noncommercial
- In pairs
- In a relationship
- Same generation
- In private
- No pornography
- Bodies only
- Vanilla

Outside the charmed circle, taking up residence on the "outer limits," Rubin locates the sexual activities that she identifies as "bad, abnormal, unnatural, damned sexuality":

- Homosexual
- Unmarried
- Promiscuous
- Non-procreative
- Commercial
- Alone or in groups
- Casual
- Cross-generational
- In public
- Pornography

- With manufactured objects
- Sadomasochistic

All of this adds up to what Rubin calls sex negativity.

Given our culture's alarmist and protectionist attitudes toward youth sexual activity, adding "sex while young" to the compendium of taboos is not a stretch. This deeply entrenched attitude is most apparent in two institutions that wield great authority in the lives of young people: the law and education. The law not only dictates when someone is old enough to consent to sexual activity; it also does not hesitate to criminalize and punish what most experts on child and adolescent health deem to be normal, natural, and healthy sexual exploration (Levine, 2002). As for education, sex education is typically an anatomy lesson embedded within a puritanism that considers "comprehensive sex education . . . a danger to moral development" (Tiefer, 2004). Education focused on "prevention" (of pregnancy, HIV and STIs, and sexual activity itself) reflects the fundamental societal belief that teen sexuality is deviant behavior (Perel, 2006), and by extension, that sexually active teens are deviants. And that's even if you're not queer.

Rubin compares these "hierarchies of sexual value" to other systems of injustice and oppression, noting how all such systems serve to justify the welfare, rights, and happiness of the privileged while rationalizing the hardships of the underclass, in this case, the "sexual rabble" (p. 280).

What's in and what's out are not fixed and permanent, however. Sexual practices previously solidly located in the bad "outer limits" later gained social sanction—albeit not without conflict.

Moreover, the acceptance of contemporary middle-class gay culture is largely reliant on unearned privileges from other social realms, such as race, class, ability, nation, and age (Jindal, 2008; Munoz, 1999; Sycamore, 2008). The intersection of these other critical markers of social location with a gay identity can render a person doubly queer, as they fail to meet societal measures of normativity in two (or more) identity areas.[3]

In resisting erotophobia and sex negativity, Rubin (1984) calls for "a radical theory of sex" (p. 275) founded on a constructionist alternative to essentialist accounts of sex. Through this lens, sex is understood to be historically and culturally contingent and constituted through relationship rather than biologically determined. The body, Rubin asserts, is never unmediated by culture.

Rubin advocates for a sexual morality that "judge(s) sexual acts by the way partners treat one another, the level of mutual consideration, the presence or absence of coercion, and the quantity and quality of the pleasures they provide" (p. 283). Such a relational ethic stands in stark contrast to the "sexual stratification and erotic persecution" (p. 288) legislated and enforced by the state, a level of governmental involvement Rubin states would not be tolerated in other domains of private life. Furthermore, by removing what amounts to state-sponsored shame, people's relationship to desire and pleasure can become a subject of productive and meaningful conversations.

Perhaps the striking shift from sex negativity to sex positivity can be found in the reworking of our understanding of children's and youth's sexuality.

DIRTY DIALOGICS: SEX POSITIVITY IN PRACTICE

What does sex positivity look like in therapeutic practice? First and foremost, a sex-positive practitioner is unfazed by, yet respectfully curious about, all matters of sex. Queer youth have told me that my engaging with them about sex without hesitation or judgment has made a helpful difference for them. Many also speak of experiences with professionals in which they felt at best ignored and at worst, exoticized, or judged.

This engaged, respectful curiosity is central to a queer relational ethic. It helps to create a discursive space that can use a variety of conversational resources. These include the following:

1. *Self-reflexive practice:* In traditional family therapy terms, this is considered part of "self-of-the-therapist" work, and involves a situated examination of one's own ideas, values, attitudes, feelings, etc., about sex, youth sex, queer youth sex, and related concerns. The purpose of this, as McNamee (2009) observes, "is to entertain doubt about our own certainties" (p. 65). This examination can involve deconstruction, discourse analysis, and meaning-making around the general question of *what's going on with me?* More specific questions one might consider include:

- *How do my reactions to, and attitudes about, queer youth and sex reflect my cultural and professional training?*
- *What discourses might be influencing my attitudes?*
- *What have been some of the messages about queer youth and sex that I have received from the media, pop culture, my culture, my religion, my professional training, my family, etc.?*
- *What have I been culturally and professionally trained to believe about youth and sex? How have I (intentionally or not) put these lessons into practice, especially in my work?*
- *What values and relational ethic do my attitudes seem to support? Is this the ethic that I want to embrace? Why or why not?*
- *What values and relational ethic do I want to practice? What changes might I make in order to practice these?*

Here's a helpful exercise: Imagine a queer youth—someone you know as a client or in your personal life—asking you these questions. Imagine yourself answering the questions as this person listens. Within the context and history of your relationship with this youth, what significance do their questions hold? How might a previous experience with this youth have been different if you had considered these questions and your answers before? How might your future conversations together be different after reflecting on these questions?

Next, review the practice vignettes in this chapter ("The Talk" and "Sex Isn't Dirty . . . Even When It's Dirty"). Take some time to reflect on the above questions in consideration of the stories in these vignettes. Where do these questions take you?

The process of self-reflection is constant and lifelong. Indeed, it is a critical component of being a competent and ethical professional. In self-reflection, we examine both the intentions and the effects of what we do. These are crucial ethical considerations. They are also powerful antidotes to complacency. Without reflection we let ourselves off the leash of accountability and head down the trail of "good enough." But our idea of "good enough" may not, in fact, been good enough for our clients.

2. *Relational reflexivity:* This is an accountability practice that involves engaging clients directly, sincerely, and consistently throughout each therapeutic conversation by asking them:

- *How is this conversation going for you?*
- *Are we talking about what you want to talk about?*
- *How is this making a difference for you? What are you getting from it?*
- *Is there something we haven't talked about that you'd like to discuss, or something I haven't asked about that you wish I would?*
- *What can we do to make this conversation more meaningful, productive, or useful for you?*

I ask these questions, and elaborations of them, throughout each therapy session. At the end of the meeting, I take time to solicit clients' feedback about their experience, focusing on what I could have done differently or what they didn't find helpful so that I can make adjustments in response to their preferences.[4] In discussions about sex, I exercise extra sensitivity and try to create a conversational climate that allows for feedback about hard-to-talk-about topics.

Below are some questions to ask relationally reflexive questions:

- *How have (or haven't) you been encouraged and trained to seek client feedback and to position their experiences and preferences at the center of your work together?*

- *What cultural and professional messages either facilitate or inhibit your seeking input from clients when discussing sex?*
- *What support do you need from your colleagues or supervisors to seek client feedback, especially in regard to conversations about sex?*
- *What do you suppose it would be like for a queer youth to have you ask them sincerely for their input? What will it be like for you to do this?*

3. *A focus on possibility and meaning-making rather than certainty:* Invite reflection rather than certitude by embracing rather than trying to fix uncertainty. Uncertainty is full of potential: it helps us unhinge the specifications of prevailing discourses and can be a vehicle for a proliferation of possible meanings. Making and keeping a flexible discursive space is especially important for conversations about sex and sexuality, as it facilitates an inclusive and affirming position. Keep in mind that often statements set forth certainties while questions call forth possibilities. Questions of curiosity born out of the conversation (vs. questions that collect information so that you may render a professional opinion) call forth the most possibilities. In the practice vignettes shared in this chapter ("The Talk" and "Sex Isn't Dirty . . . Even When It's Dirty"), what "certainties" are challenged? In what ways are possibility and meaning-making foci of the conversations? Where may you have been inclined to make a statement rather than ask a curious question? What other questions would you ask to unhinge certainty, invite possibilities, or focus on meaning-making?

4. *A situated understanding of individual narratives:* Remember that all individual narratives are located within the discursive context of larger cultural narratives. Ignoring the influences of cultural narratives on people's stories decontextualizes their lives and can lead to thin conclusions. It can also privatize social problems. This can be particularly problematic with a marginalized group such as queer youth with a culturally proscribed topic such as sex.

Try this: Tell a story about yourself. It can be about anything—your professional self, activities you enjoy, political beliefs, a vacation you took, and so forth. Try to tell it without communicating *anything* that connects you (even implicitly) to other people, institutions, broader cultural ideas, etc. What happens to the meaning of your story?

Now, tell a story about yourself involving a personal sexual matter or encounter. Is it possible for *your* story to have the meaning you want it to if it's divorced from the cultural meanings specific to its time and location? Bring your storytelling experiences to the matter of queer youth sex. What are the cultural stories that may impact the individual stories of queer youth in matters of sex? What cultural narratives impact you as a professional in your work with queer youth around matters of sex?

5. *Multiple perspectives:* Invite a multiplicity of perspectives to encourage a diversity of understandings. These perspectives can include family (however it may be defined) friends, mentors, and other people important to your client, whether real or imagined, dead or alive. Entertaining multiple perspectives is another way to invite possibilities and challenge specifications. Further, by inviting meaningful and appreciative others into the conversation, sex can often be discussed in more open and liberatory ways.

In seeking multiple perspectives, I often use re-membering practices (Myerhoff, 1978, 1982, 1986).[5] These practices, from narrative therapy, (Hedtke, 2001a, 2001b, 2003; Hedtke & Winslade, 2004; Russell & Carey, 2002; White, 1988, 2007) are based on the idea that the people in our lives contribute to the stories we use to organize our identities and lives. The people whom we want to contribute to our preferred stories can be granted "membership" to our lives, and we re-member them when we intentionally seek their contributions and center them in our lives.

For example, I have many teachers and mentors whose ideas, perspectives, and support I rely on when doing therapy, training others, or writing. When I feel stuck or unsure, or when I am told by others that I am not clear or helpful, I often think about how some of these important people may advise me about the situation, how they may think about it, or what they may do. It's my own personal, reflective "What Would (fill in the blank) Do?" bracelet. What's more, I don't have to limit myself to "real" people. I have granted membership to important and inspirational people of all sorts—even those whom I have never met personally (such as the many theorists I have cited in this book).

In the vignettes in this chapter ("The Talk" and "Sex Isn't Dirty . . . Even When It's Dirty"), what are some re-membering questions? What are some others that you might ask? Whom do you want to re-member into your professional life? Your personal life? Whose influences do you want on how you think about sex and the queer youth you work with?

6. *A Storied embodiment of experience:* Be sure to invite stories—not simply "facts"—so that people's accounts of themselves are rich, situated, and contextualized. In conversations about sex, it is important to do this with sophistication and sensitivity, so as to avoid a voyeuristic quality. Ask about meanings, reflections, preferences, and hopes; this encourages stories that can be told with dignity and heard with respect.

For example, consider the vignette "Sex Isn't Dirty . . . Even When It's Dirty." If we deconstruct the story as I've conveyed it, we could break it down into "facts," such as: Anthony and Joe have been dating for several months; they decided to have sex; the encounter was enjoyable until afterward, when Anthony was grossed out by the dirty sheets, etc.

If I had listed these "facts" without situating them within the broader contexts of Anthony and Joe's developing relationship, the cultural meanings that resonate with the two young men, and the feelings they experienced, how would you have understood the story? Would it have even felt like a story to you?

Finally, think of a time in your own life when someone focused on "just the facts" and ignored the totality and richness of your experience that brought those "facts" to life with meaning. What was that like for you?

7. *Attention to temporal dimension:* Facilitate conversations that travel fluidly through past, present, and future (imaginary) temporal domains, and that seek to locate and articulate how new meanings, preferences, or actions have taken (or may take) place across time. Youth's desires and the meanings they make of them can change and *that* they change may be as significant as the stuff of the change. Remember when you were first learning how to write and you were given the basic guidelines of storytelling: *who, what, when, where, and why*? Our conversations are stories and attention to the temporal dimension—the *when*—can be a rich source of meaning-making.

As an example, here is a brief excerpt of a conversation with Justin, an HIV-positive, queer, eighteen-year-old youth. During this conversation, we took inventory of our work together over the previous eight months. In this particular exchange, we focused on this "time travel," underscoring not only what has happened (or has yet to happen) but also on *when* it happened (or might happen).

> *Justin:* I totally have been talking back to HIV[6] whenever it tries to keep me from even just meeting other guys or getting to know them. I've told it to back off—I'm just trying to socialize and I get to be sexual again if I want to be.
>
> *Julie:* Justin, when would you say you first started talking back to HIV in such a strong voice, particularly around dating and sex?
>
> *Justin:* Probably, I'd say, maybe like the last month or so.
>
> *Julie:* If we were to go back, say, four, six, eight months ago, and I had said to you, "You know, Justin, in a few months you're going to be interested again in meeting guys and maybe thinking about being sexual again," what would you have said?
>
> *Justin:* That you weren't listening to me and that's insane. I wouldn't have even been able to think about it. I was so depressed and focused on the [HIV] diagnosis.
>
> *Julie:* Given how unthinkable it would have been a few months ago, how depressed you were feeling, and how focused on HIV you were, what is the significance of your talking back to HIV about these things today?

Justin: It's really significant. Big-time, huge.

Julie: What would you say are some of the big-time huge things about this eight-month turnabout?

Justin (tearfully): Well, it's like I'm free to think about having a life—a relationship and sexual life. When I was first diagnosed, I couldn't have imagined that—I didn't think I was deserving or that anyone would be interested in me. So, yeah, that's big-time—I feel worthwhile again, of a relationship. And I never thought I would.

Julie: Justin, if you were to imagine us sitting together talking another four, six, eight months down the road from now, what do you suppose you will be telling me that you've been doing that is unthinkable today?

Justin: You mean, eight months from now what will I be doing that I don't think is even a possibility today?

Julie: Yeah, that's right.

Justin: Well, part of me would say being in a relationship and feeling good about it and being healthy, because I suppose HIV still tells me I can't do that, or have that. But, now that you ask that, there's a part of me that thinks we just might have that talk . . . maybe not in eight months, but sometime down the road.

Julie: What do you think it says about you and your struggle to take your life back from HIV that you've made these changes and that you are imagining more changes?

Justin (tearfully): That I'm here for the long haul. And HIV may get its shots in, but it's not going to tell me who I am forever. I wouldn't have said that even four months ago.

SEX ISN'T DIRTY . . . EVEN WHEN IT'S DIRTY: A CASE VIGNETTE

Anthony was a nineteen-year-old Native American college freshman. He was referred by a classmate and friend of his, a former client of mine. Anthony said that he wanted someone to talk to about the many transitions he was experiencing: living on campus at a large public university after growing up near the reservation in a rural part of the state; being one of just a few indigenous people on campus; finding his way—literally and metaphorically—at school, in the city, and within the much more "out" community he found himself in; and negotiating the multitude of choices about classes, careers, priorities, identity, relationships, etc.

Anthony and I talked over the course of several weeks about all of those things. One day, Anthony said he "had to ask me something but didn't really want to talk about it." I said that that could be tricky and wondered if there were other ways besides talking that we could approach his question. We talked about talking about it—without naming "it," the thing he wanted to ask about. Together we wondered what it would be like to talk about it, what he hoped to come of it, what was standing between us that kept us from talking, the implications of NOT talking about it, etc. This opened up space for Anthony to talk about it.

Anthony said he had some "worries" about a recent sexual encounter with Joe, the young man he had been seeing for several months. His cousin Angela had introduced him to Joe at her birthday party. They hit it off right away and Anthony and Joe had been dating since. Like Anthony, Joe, who was European American, was a college student, but he had much more sexual experience than Anthony.

Anthony described his feelings about Joe and their developing relationship. "I'm like so totally into him, more than anyone I've dated before," he beamed. "And, it's not just like, about sex, 'cuz we been kickin' it for a while before, you know, we started doing more stuff. We both like music and he likes to draw and so do I and we both are involved at the queer student centers at our schools, we do our homework together sometimes, and I totally trust him and he tells me stuff about his life. And for a white boy from the city, well, he isn't all 'Indian this and Indian that.' You know, my cousin hooked us up and she's too smart to hang out with anyone sketchy. And my roommate and other friends like him, too."

I reflected back the excitement I heard in his voice about finding someone who brought so much to his life. Then I asked him what he could tell me about the worries that were troubling him.

His response was a teary and frightened gaze into my eyes.

I wondered aloud what effect the worries were having on this young love. "Anthony," I asked, "are these worries about your sexual experience with Joe worries that should be listened to because they can help keep you safe in the relationship, or . . . are they worries that are getting you to doubt the relationship for no good reason, or . . . are they worries that come from someone else's ideas or messages about what is and isn't OK, or . . . Are they some other kind of worry? These are just some possibilities. How would you describe what these worries are?"

"Probably some of all of that," Anthony said.

Anthony described having anal intercourse with Joe, during which Anthony "topped" Joe. He said that he really wanted to be sexual in this way with Joe (who had experience with anal sex), that they used condoms, that early in their relationship they had STI/HIV tests, and that they had "talked about it for weeks and did other stuff to like, you know, get ready." He shared the story of a romantic date that included a walk along the river, the exchange of small gifts while sitting in a park, and sharing ice cream. Anthony said everything was "perfect" until the encounter was over. When Joe excused himself to get some water and change the music that was playing, Anthony noticed on the sheets that there were "skid marks."

Embarrassed, Anthony puzzled over this. "Joe talked about how he, well, I guess, you know, cleaned up beforehand. But it just kind of freaked me out. When he came back and brought me some water he was all sweet and cuddly and I wanted to be close but at the same time I didn't."

"So," I said, "everything—the walk, the gifts, all the time building and connecting in the relationship over the last few months—everything up to being sexual and *including* being sexual was perfect, you said?"

"Yeah, *totally*. It was just when I saw, you know . . . shit."

We talked about what was or wasn't surprising about this. Anthony explained, chuckling a little, that "in my head I knew that shit happens," but that the reality of it brought forward ideas that he thought he had long ago set aside, ideas about "gay sex being wrong and bad and, dirty." These, he said, were the worries that were causing him difficulty, distracting him not only when he was with Joe, but also when his thoughts would wander at other times during his day.

I checked with Anthony to see how he was doing with our conversation, making sure that he wasn't experiencing any kind of judgment or surveillance from me. I asked him if it would be OK to ask about the specific worries and ideas that were leading him to question, as he put it, "how I enjoy myself."

Here are some of the questions that Anthony and I considered together:

- *What would your body say about these worries?*
- *What do you think of the fact that our bodies are capable of bringing us such pleasure and such disgust?*
- *What influences your ideas about what is pleasing and what is gross? Are these "natural" and experienced the same by everyone everywhere?*
- *If having anal sex is so gross and wrong, how do you explain that all kinds of people (gay and straight, married with children, young and old, etc.) engage in it?*
- *In your relationship with Joe, what place do you want disgust to have?*
- *Considering everything that your relationship is about and what you hope it will become, what is most important to you in terms of your sexual relationship with Joe?*
- *Who would benefit from two young queer lovers having their relationship end over something like this?*

- *What are some of the negative stories you've heard told about anal sex? What are the positive stories? Who tells which ones? Why do you think that's the case?*
- *When you consider who tells the negative stories and who tells the positive stories about anal sex, which storytellers do you want to listen to? Why?*
- *When you've watched sex scenes in movies (mainstream or porn) or looked at other media representations of any kind of sex acts, how dirty did they get? What part do these antiseptic media portrayals play in your idea of how sex is supposed to be?*
- *Whose ideas or voices are behind these ideas or worries that this isn't okay? Are these the ideas or voices that you want to take to bed with you and Joe?*
- *How have you dealt with other kinds of shit in your life?*
- *Whose experience or advice would you find helpful? What do you imagine they might say about these worries?*

These questions helped create some space for Anthony to consider what cultural messages he was being influenced by and which discourses or voices he would prefer to help shape his ideas about sex and his relationship to it. It was not my agenda to challenge his experience of being grossed out or the idea that shit is gross, or to convince him of anything in particular. Rather, I was creating a conversation that allowed him to consider and experience the complexities at hand. I was interested in situating his local experience within the larger social and political culture of messages about sex, anal sex, youth sex, queer youth sex, etc., thus connecting his individual story with influential cultural narratives. Further, I was interested in multiplying the perspectives available to him so he could consider what he wanted to influence his story of sex and his relationship to it. Part of our conversation involved the possibility of not engaging in anal sex at all (a choice made by many people). Anthony was clear that he wanted to find a way to "be okay with it, because I really liked it . . . and so does Joe."

We discussed how he and Joe dealt with Anthony's reaction. He explained that Joe was understanding and patient but that "he really wanted me to see that it was no big deal. He kept saying, 'Is it worth it to get upset over some dirty sheets when we had such a great time together?'"

I asked Anthony how he answered Joe's question. Anthony chuckled and said that at the time, he said, "No, it isn't worth it," but that he couldn't see "how to get there." Now, after our conversation, Anthony said he felt as though the "how to get there" was about "remembering why I am with Joe, in the relationship, in the first place."

As Anthony and Joe continued to develop their relationship, we had further conversations that explored his sexual preferences and the values he wanted to bring to their relationship. Joe joined us for a few sessions, and we had rich conversations about how being young queer men engaging in a mutually caring, responsible, and sex-positive relationship challenged many cultural rules and ideas about youth sexuality and men in relationships. This helped them feel a shared commitment to their relationship and a sex-positive stance. Anthony and Joe also identified friends they knew who supported their relationship and embraced a sex-positive position. They agreed that having conversations with these friends and participating in sex-positive community programs helped them live into their own visions of sexuality.

Together, they negotiated ways to talk about what was and wasn't okay sexually. They named one of their strategies "shit-talk," which meant that they agreed to talk together about shit—real and metaphorical—in their relationship so that the shit didn't do the talking for them.

THE TALK: A CASE VINGETTE

Cheryl, a thirty-eight-year-old African American pediatric nurse, and her fourteen-year-old daughter Alicia had met with me three times over six weeks. Cheryl was parenting Alicia alone; her husband, Alicia's dad, was killed in a car accident when Alicia was three. They originally sought therapy after Alicia "came out," first to her aunt Toni, Cheryl's lesbian older sister, and then to Cheryl. They were interested in addressing issues related to the climate at Alicia's school. Cheryl and Alicia were concerned about the capacity of school personnel to create a safe, inclusive climate for Alicia and other LGBT and queer-identified students.

During our fourth meeting we took inventory of everything they had done to bring their concerns forward until they felt confident that Alicia's school would be inclusive of and responsive to LGBT and queer students. I commented (and Alicia agreed) that Cheryl was a good mom, one to be reckoned with should anyone threaten her kid.

Cheryl breathed a heavy sigh. "You know, this *has* been good. I've got some good plans on how to keep Alicia safe and keep the school people doing the right things. Alicia is feeling good about it, too, wouldn't you say?"

Alicia nodded. "Yeah, I think that Mr. Hawkins, Mr. Anderson, and Mrs. Mattson know what's what. And the GSA is cool—I didn't think I'd want to do that but I like the meetings and stuff."

Cheryl added, "But there's something that kind of came up and surprised me that I'm feeling really, well, disappointed or sad about. And it's not you, honey, it's about me." She looked at Alicia and put her hand on her puzzled daughter's shoulder. "I'm sad as a mom of a daughter because now I can't give her 'the talk.'"

As Alicia rolled her eyes and squirmed with embarrassment, I found myself touched by the sweet earnestness of Cheryl's embrace of this particular mother's duty. I asked Cheryl what it was about being the mom of a daughter that held special meaning for her around giving The Talk.

Cheryl described how her aunt Sarah, who had raised her, had been especially deliberate in talking with her about "my body and how to take care of it and the gifts it brings."

As we talked, it became clear that what Cheryl meant by The Talk was not the mechanics of sex or anything unique to *heterosexual* sexual acts. What she wanted to convey to her daughter was valuable regardless of Alicia's identity or desires. Cheryl's Talk was about values and meaning, about being a self-respecting woman, proud of her body and its capacity to experience and give sexual pleasure without shame or judgment from others.

Here are some of the questions that I asked Cheryl about her intention, hopes, and values that she wished to communicate to Alicia:

- *What would you hope your daughter most understands about what it means to be in a sexual relationship with another person?*
- *What about that is important to you? Who helped you learn its importance?*
- *What advice would Aunt Sarah give you to give to Alicia about being proud of her body?*
- *How has Alicia already demonstrated herself to be free of shame? What gives you confidence that she will carry on this way? Would you say she is already on her way to learning from you and Sarah?*
- *Can you say something about what makes it so important —and special— for you to have The Talk with your daughter? How is this part of your mission as a mom?*
- *If you were to give a title to The Talk, or come up with a phrase that captures the spirit of it, what would that be?*
- *If you imagine Alicia someday being a parent or an aunt to another young woman, what will Alicia share with that young person that lets you know she has taken your words to heart?*

I was also interested in exposing what led her to think that The Talk would no longer be relevant because Alicia was queer. We also discussed how her experience as the mom of a queer youth challenged the prevailing cultural messages that we were uncovering together. Here are some of the questions that I asked:

- *As we consider what matters most to you about The Talk, would you say that these things hold their significance regardless of whom Alicia may choose to be with?*
- *What do you make of that? Does it surprise you or does it make sense somehow?*

- *What led you to think that the wisdom you had to share with your daughter wasn't useful because she is queer? What—or whose—ideas and assumptions are behind this?*
- *Do these assumptions reflect the spirit of what Aunt Sarah taught you as a young woman?*
- *What would Aunt Sarah change, if anything, about The Talk if she were to give it to Alicia or any other queer youth?*
- *In what ways might our culture ignore the parents of nonheterosexual kids?*
- *What are some of the consequences—good, bad, or benign—of all this for the parents of queer kids?*
- *How would you hope that giving Alicia The Talk today might change the way things are for queer kids and their parents tomorrow?*

As we talked, Cheryl acknowledged that she had become "misdirected" from her intentions by ideas of "the specifics of sex." She was relieved to realize that what she most wanted to say to Alicia was still relevant, commenting that she hoped "someday she will understand that I mean it to be something special we've talked about." Alicia, relieved to avoid "another one of those science talks," said that she would prefer to hear what her mom had to say at home, without me there. I agreed that this sounded like a private mom-daughter talk. Cheryl was touched that Alicia was open to having this conversation.

Cheryl explained that she in fact had "talked about the birds and bees, the sex-ed stuff" a few times with Alicia since she was a little girl. We discussed how this information was still important, as sexual anatomy, reproduction, birth control, STIs and HIV, and being in charge of one's own body were all issues that every young person needed to know about. Alicia, insisting that she "only likes girls" (and reporting that she had yet to be sexually active at all) resisted the idea that knowing about birth control and "boy's junk" were necessary. I explained that queer kids do get pregnant and get others pregnant (Forest & Saewyc, 2004; Saewyc et al., 1999; 2008). This didn't move her much, but she did agree that knowing about such things may be useful for her as a friend to straight kids.

As for STIs and HIV, both Cheryl and I were clear that Alicia needed to know about safer sex practices and how these diseases are and are not transmitted. I explained that STIs and HIV did not only infect gay men and straight people, and that when she was ready to be sexual with another girl, they would need to know how to keep themselves safer. We discussed how and from whom she would prefer to learn this information. As a nurse, Cheryl felt qualified to share information about disease transmission and the tools and techniques of safer sex. Alicia tried to veto this idea: "You may be a nurse, but you're not *my* nurse; you're my *mom!*" We came to a negotiated agreement: Cheryl would have the "science talk" (the fourteen-year-old queer-sex version) with Alicia, providing information about disease transmission and protection strategies. She would also direct Alicia to some resources (written materials and websites) that she knew to have accurate information. The negotiation involved Cheryl's agreement that she wouldn't ask Alicia any specific questions about her sexual interests or activities; rather, Alicia asked her to "present all the stuff like she was teaching it in front of a big class of students." We also left open the option of Alicia being able to meet with me alone to talk about relationships and sex, and to accept her aunt Toni's offer to talk if she wanted to do so.

As we wrapped up our conversation, Alicia thanked Cheryl for being "a cool mom." Cheryl laughed, gave her daughter a hug, and thanked her for being a cool daughter. I thanked them both for teaching me how to be cool about something hot like sex.

NOTES

1. For more in-depth analysis of how capitalism co-opts social change movements, see Habermas (1991) and Jameson (1991).
2. See the appendix for a list of resources for sex-positive literature and organizations serving youth.
3. For a more thorough analysis of intersectionality and analysis from a queer people of color perspective, see Sycamore (2008).
4. I formalize this by using feedback forms to monitor outcome and alliance. This is the process of feedback informed treatment. For more information, see ICCE Group (2012).
5. Other practices that invite multiple perspectives that I frequently use also include circular questioning (Penn, 1982; Selvini et al., 1980; Tomm, 1987, 1988) and internalized other interviews (Epston, 1993; Tomm, Hoyt, & Madigan, 1998). Because this book is not a "how-to" book of techniques, my purpose here is to focus on the theoretical and relational positioning of queer theory and social construction. The reader is free to try on a variety of practices to bring these ideas to life.
6. Justin and I had externalized HIV.

Chapter Six

iQueer

Popular Culture and Therapeutic Moments

Media and communications are central elements of modern life, whilst gender and sexuality remain at the core of how we think about our identities.

—David Gauntlett, media studies scholar

I take a lot of inspiration for expressing my queerness through fashion and media.

—Ruben, Q-Squad member

I AM WHAT I OWN

As I write this, I am typing on my Mac laptop, keyboard illuminated by a desk lamp with Apple, Incorporated's logo affixed to the lamp's base. (You wouldn't catch me owning a PC in a million years. Eww.) *I am comfortable in my hoodie and vintage ringer T-shirt. I kick off my Chuckie-Ts and let my toes stretch into my socks.* (My students think the shirt is cool.) *The Americano I picked up on the way home from the third-wave coffee shop down the street is about gone now, having spilled a few ounces as I hip-checked closed the door to my MINI Cooper.* (Who *was* I before I had this car???) *My cats, Presto and Juno* (named, respectively, for the Pixar short that accompanied WALL-E and the film starring Ellen Page) *begin tearing the cover of the latest issue of* Rolling Stone *that I left on the floor. Ushering them out of the room, I close the door to keep out the sound of the TV from distracting me. (*Damn! She's watching *Glee*! I never have time to watch that anymore.) *I close Skype so I'm not distracted by anyone looking to visit me while I try to work.* (I've kept Facebook open, knowing that the possibility that someone may pop up in a chat box is pretty good.) *I clear the clutter from my desk: iPod, iPhone, and drawings of ideas for my next tattoo.* (It's been over a year since I had new ink . . . I'm itching for ink!) *I was right. My hip-hop junkie friend opens a chat box and wants to know if I want to go see a cool MC who's in town tomorrow night.* (Wouldn't miss it.)

Popular and media culture have assumed hegemonic status in contemporary North American society (Nylund, 2007; Tilsen & Nylund, 2009). Therapists and counselor educators Monk, Winslade, and Sinclair (2008) argue that media culture is "perhaps the most powerful cultural force shaping cultural identity today" (p. 243). Consequently, any treatment of identity and therapeutic practice would be remiss if it failed to consider the influence—both problematic and productive—of popular culture in people's lives.

> *I feel very close and personal to my music. When I share it with people and they don't enjoy it, it can feel very offensive. I feel like that's a very close thing to me and if you don't like that, then, do you like me?*
>
> —Dylan, Q-Squad member

In this chapter, I do not critique specific popular culture representations from a queer theory perspective;[1] rather, my focus is on (1) discussing the significance of pop culture to identity construction; (2) introducing cultural studies methods as a theoretical ally to queer theory and narrative therapy practice (Nylund, 2007; Tilsen & Nylund, 2012); and, (3) exploring ways in which pop culture has influenced the lives of the Q-Squad and my clients, and how these youth influence the texts by queering them.

Barker (2000) observes that the industries that produce and disseminate culture provide the very stuff that individuals use to construct identities. The culture industries create a world that is saturated by corporate-sponsored messages, both implicit and explicit about gender, race, class, nationality, sexuality, and ethnicity (Tilsen & Nylund, 2009). Indeed, Monk et al. (2008) suggest that, for contemporary youth, the messages and values of mass media have eclipsed those traditionally provided by families and cultural communities. Put another way, horizontal culture (circulated by peer groups) has become more important than vertical culture (passed on through multiple family generations).[2] These powerful and ubiquitous messages persuade people to follow the dominant discourses both reflected in and produced by pop culture (Miller, 2001). These discourses include:

- Capitalism/consumerism
- Beauty/body specifications
- Patriarchy
- Hegemonic masculinity

- Whiteness
- Ableism
- Heteronormativity/homonormativity

> *What do you do with that experience of not seeing yourself represented? A lot of that can be unhealthy, self-destructive behaviors.*
>
> —Courtney, Q-Squad member

Queer youth have to contend with all of these discourses, just as people from other social locations do. Increasingly, they experience popular culture's propagation of homonormative messages and images. For example, shows such as "Queer as Folk," "The L Word," "Will and Grace," and "Queer Eye for the Straight Guy" appear to challenge heteronormative discourses by bringing gay men and lesbians into people's living rooms without limiting them to their traditional roles of comic relief, sexual psychopaths, or social misfits. Yet, these shows present a largely white, middle-class, consumption-oriented image of "queer" people. They also uphold the homo/hetero binary. These shows uphold both heteronormativity and homonormativity. Indeed, calling these shows and their characters "queer" is a misnomer, as their representations are anchored within the normative systems of apolitical domesticity and consumption that defines homonormativity.

As a therapist, I am interested in how queer youth experience pop culture's presence in their lives, as well as in how they mediate those effects in order to reach preferred—and queered—meanings.

Media and popular culture do not selectively influence queer youth. Adults (including therapists) have no special immunity to the seduction of fashion flavors, techno toys, media mania, virtual visiting, or any of the other products and promises of popular culture machinery. Indeed, even as we roll our eyes at the fashion choices of young people, we forget to look at the labels on our own clothing. Consider the following questions about your relationship—past and present—with pop culture:

- *Think back to your childhood and adolescence. What movies, TV shows, music, and other popular culture products did you consume?*
- *What meaning(s) did you make of your relationship with popular culture? What role did it play in the shaping of your identity?*
- *Did you identify with a particular character? A particular song? In what ways did that character or song help you through a challenging time?*
- *What messages about your pop culture interests did you receive from the important adults in your life?*
- *In what ways does your relationship with popular culture influence you today?*

- *As an adult, how have your consumption patterns changed or stayed the same? How has the meaning you make of what you consume in popular culture changed or stayed the same?*

MEANING, INC.: A CULTURAL STUDIES–INFORMED PRACTICE

I think it's super harmful when you don't analyze pop culture.
—Ruben, Q-Squad member

The relationship consumers have with the culture industries has changed as technology (both a driving force and central product of popular culture) has changed. This is especially true for young people, who interact with technology like no generation before (Gauntlett, 2008). This change involves the shift from *audience* to *user* or *participant* (although Gauntlett smartly suggests that the notion of audience now "incorporates a level of interactivity" [p. 2]).

The defining question about this interactivity centers on power and influence: Does pop culture wield unchallenged influence over people, or do people ultimately maintain some power over the texts it produces? The first position is best articulated by Horkheimer and Adorno (2002) and Adorno (1991), who argue that the culture industries exert ultimate power over people who remain passive in their uncritical consumption of mass-produced images. The latter argument is represented by Fiske (1989a, 1989b), who asserts that people not only consume popular culture, they also produce it. That is, the audience, in its interactive capacity, holds the power of interpretation. This interpretive agency, *situated within a person's relationship with media texts*, undergirds the interdisciplinary field of cultural studies. It is this process of situated activity that interests me and that influences my work as a therapist and youth worker.

Fiske argues that, because people construct individual, fluid meanings about the cultural texts they interact with, a homogenous constituency—"the consumers"—is not a meaningful concept. Rather, people interact with these texts as they do with many things in their lives: in complex, dynamic ways that reflect the uniqueness and multiplicity of their identities and the social locations they occupy. Consequently, while artifacts of pop culture may contain a text (or texts) intended by their original producers, they "also offer possibilities for consumers to create their own alternative or resistant readings" (Gauntlett, 2008, p. 28). Hall (1997)—upon whose work Fiske's has expanded—also points to the connection between representations (cultural products) and audiences (meanings made) by theorizing "identity as constituted, not outside, but within representation" (p. 58). Because popular culture provides materials from which we may construct our identities, Hall suggests that in doing so we may recreate ourselves in multiple and new ways, thus occupying new positions “from which to speak” (1997, p. 58). This speaking can even include a resistant voice to the influence of mass media and consumer culture—one that I often invite into therapeutic conversations as an ally for clients’ preferred selves.

In what ways does the field of cultural studies provide resources for creating these kinds of conversations with young people? As a critical field of inquiry informed by multicultural and constructionist ideas, cultural studies provides a conceptual framework for reading media texts from a variety of perspectives (Kellner, 1995). Of particular interest is developing media literacy skills. These shed light on how dominant values and power relations are encoded within the texts of pop culture. Illumination of these prevailing discourses and the ways in which the culture industries work to manipulate consumers “can empower individuals to negotiate the dominant meanings in media cultural products and to produce their own meanings” (Tilsen & Nylund, 2009, p. 7).

Thus, critique, contradiction, and resistance may be developed and leveraged toward pursuit of a more critical and intentional relationship with media culture. This “reading against the grain” allows people to negotiate their own meanings for their own purposes.

For example, the production and wearing of clothes specifically marketed to young African American men may be read as a way to contest white, middle-class values of appropriateness by constructing identity through fashion and economic solidarity. Another example is young queers who perform gender representations in ways that contest compulsory heteronormativity through fashion and body art. In both examples, the fashion industry—a cultural site heavy with texts reinforcing white, middle-class, hetero- and homonormative consumer values—is used as a way to challenge dominant texts and produce situated countertexts that account for power relations by seeing political agency in the consumer-audience.

Cultural studies involve analysis in three domains (Ang, 1996): *political economy*, an analysis of the production and distribution of popular culture; *textual analysis* of the messages encoded within media texts;[3] and the *meanings* that audiences make of the popular culture texts (researched with audience reception studies). These three domains can help shape therapeutic conversations. There is no formula for asking them in a particular order. What is asked, when it is asked, how it is asked, and if it is asked at all depend on the specific therapeutic conversation.

Let’s look at each of these domains more closely. I work with queer youth grappling with hetero- and homonormative images. I investigate the *political economy* of a media text with them by asking these questions:

- *Whom do you imagine is responsible for creating these images of happy heterosexual couples?*

- *What companies own the TV shows that depict gays and lesbians within the male/female, homo/hetero binaries?*
- *If you were a consultant to these companies what kinds of changes in these images would you advise?*

Of course, youth are not likely to know who owns the production company for *Grey's Anatomy*, for example. That is not the point of this line of inquiry. While this kind of conversation often does inspire youth to research these things, the idea is to open space to consider that the images they consume reflect particular values—and, importantly, that even as a consumer, one can exercise agency over those values.

For example, Kendra, a sixteen-year-old white queer-identified girl, was a big fan of Harry Potter. However, she felt very frustrated by "all the boy-girl pairings" and the "total straightness of Hogwarts." Kendra observed wisely, "If any school should be cool with a queer couple, it totally should be Hogwarts." Kendra herself had been part of a group of upper-class students at her own high school that had challenged the heterosexual status quo around dances, paving the way for queer youth to attend school events safely. She acknowledged that her current participation in these activities had heightened her awareness of the media images she was consuming. "I never really thought about it before we started challenging it at school. Now I see it in every show I watch and it pisses me off!"

I asked her, "Who is it that may be responsible for such a limited representation of Hogwarts students?" Kendra thought for a moment and replied, "Well, I suppose it's J.K. Rowling, the author." I asked, "Why do you suppose she left out the possibility of queer kids at Hogwarts?" Kendra answered, "Because that makes the straight masses uncomfortable and they may not buy the books or go to the movies." I asked Kendra to explain further. "Well, people want to see things or read about things that they recognize, I suppose. It makes them feel like they count if they can see themselves in stuff."

When I asked Kendra what she would say to Rowling or the movie producers if she had a chance, she said, "Well, I suppose I could show them the fan fiction I've been writing where Hogwarts is a queer school that teaches the students the powers of queer." Then she described her rewritten world: All of the witches and wizards were queer and went by the all-gender term *wichards*. Muggles were straight people whom the wichards befriend and look after, often using their unique "powers of queer" to help them. Voldemort and his followers, including the Death Eaters, were "homophobic and racist and against poor people and others not like them." Voldemort's agenda was to "make everyone the same—nothing unique or unusual or surprising about anyone . . . ever." I commented that that seemed to be an agenda of consumer culture and wondered if she agreed. "That's why I write fan fiction—to make things that are different."

Kendra's political economy analysis of Harry Potter revealed her awareness of the socio-political-economic machinations that drive the production of media images. Kendra brilliantly critiqued dominant practices of and meanings generated by the culture industry. She also articulated possible alternatives. And she did all of this by participating in another aspect of contemporary popular culture—fan fiction.

Textual analysis, the second domain of cultural studies, invites discussion about the values and messages encoded within specific media texts. For example:

- *What relationships seem to be approved of or celebrated in these ads?*
- *According to this film how many ways are there to be a man or a woman? What are the rules of manhood or womanhood?*
- *What do these shows imply about who you are and how you prefer to be?*
- *What message do you think the fashion industry wants you to get from the styles they offer young women?*
- *What ideas about relationships do you get after listening to these songs?*

In my conversation with Kendra, we analyzed the heteronomative messages in Harry Potter. Kendra was particularly concerned with how girls and women were portrayed. "At first," she said, "it really bugged me that Hermione seemed downplayed compared to Harry and Ron. It got better, but why did this have to be about Harry? Why couldn't Hermione—or even a genderqueer person—be the star?" I asked her how she might answer her own questions, and what she thought about the way roles were cast and gendered. "Well, they say it's a man's world, you know." I asked her how that idea being broadcast through best-selling books and blockbuster movies impacted her. She sighed. "You know, sometimes it's tiring. As a girl and as a queer person, not seeing yourself . . . Or seeing yourself only in certain kinds of ways. But then it pisses me off and makes me want to fight it." I asked, "Do you think the message of these images is intended to inspire you to fight or to go along with it?" "Oh," Kendra replied, "they want us to go along with it, I'm sure."

"So," I said, "given that you're fighting it and not just going along with it, that you're writing back and not just reading, how well are these media messages landing with you? I mean, would you say that you're being the kind of girl that they want you to be?"

Laughing, Kendra replied, "Not hardly! I'm not *that* kind of girl!"

Finally, the third domain of a cultural studies methodology includes questions to open discursive space for individual *meaning-making,* and potential transgressive readings of media texts include:

- *Despite these heteronormative and homonormative messages, what is it about the show that you like? What keeps you watching?*
- *Have you inserted yourself into the story or otherwise come up with some different versions of the story?*
- *What are some experiences in your life that may influence how you think about this?*
- *What are some things you've learned from the characters in this book?*

Kendra was clear about her love of Harry Potter even as she tempered it with her queer and feminist critiques. She loved the magic and the wonder of it, finding it all "very clever and very queer." When I asked her if she could elaborate on how she experienced it as queer, she said, "When I first read the stories, the images I got of how Professors Dumbledore and McGonagall were dressed just seemed like, well, like *drag!* And the way that people who were different were made fun of, like how Harry was hidden away by his aunt and uncle. When the movies came out, it was totally like what I had seen in my head—everyone in costumes like a big gay Halloween party!"

I told Kendra that I had what might seem like a weird question. "I'm wondering if you ever put yourself into the story—either into the Harry Potter stories themselves, or into the fan fiction you write? I know that might sound weird, but it's totally something that people do!"

"Yeah, in fact I do," Kendra said. "I thought it was weird. People do that?"

"Uh-huh—there's even a technical eggheady word for it," I said. "It's called textual poaching.[4] It's when you insert yourself in a story. It could be a movie or TV show, a story or song lyric, whatever. Totally not weird," I explained.

Kendra described how she first started seeing herself as Hermione, especially as Hermione emerged as "the smart girl that others overlooked." Then, Kendra became "Hermione's friend who worked with her." She explained that before she started writing fan fiction, she had constructed a fairly elaborate "imaginary world that felt real to me," in which she had relationships with everyone at Hogwarts.

I asked Kendra, "Who do you get to be when you are Hermione's friend that you can't be in our routine muggle world?" "I can make good things happen for people that need them." This opened a conversation about Kendra's commitment to social justice and her belief that "we all have something we can help someone with." I asked her what she had learned about justice during her time at Hogwarts. "I learned from Dobby[5] about class stuff—I hadn't thought a lot about that before." I asked, "Having had these experiences as a member of the Hogwarts world and as a writer of the world you've created, what are your plans for working toward justice here in this world?" Without pausing, Kendra said, "I want to be a writer and write about people that aren't usually the main characters. And then I might make it into a movie!"

The vignettes from my conversations with Kendra demonstrate the use of a cultural studies methodology. Often, this focus on youth's engagement with popular culture weaves in and out of the larger conversation, connecting to other concerns and themes that make up the fabric of our therapeutic work. I listen for and respond to youth's relationships with artifacts of pop culture because often these relationships are substantive and significant, carrying the possibility for meaningful identity construction and critical readings of media texts.[6]

Does this mean there are *no* concerns about harmful affects of pop culture? Engaging queer youth in meaningful conversations about their relationship with the culture industries is not meant to tacitly approve of every product sold to and consumed by young people. Nor is it meant to suggest that all consumers are (or can be) immune to the pressures and values of Madison Avenue. Hall (1980) urges caution against overestimating consumers' capacity for resistant meaning-making in the face of the powerful culture industry machine. Indeed, I am concerned about the targeting of youth as a special market; about the values of violence, consumption, and competition that pervade our mass media; and about the racialized, gendered, and sexualized qualities of popular culture products and images.

But what I am most concerned about (and where I feel I can have immediate, day-to-day, conversation-to-conversation impact in youth's lives) is the binary construction of the typical discourse about popular culture. One response is a moral panic that implies that youth are hollow dupes "incapable of negotiating meaning, lacking the capacity for critical discernment, and destined to be forever negatively affected by the things they consume" (Tilsen & Nylund, 2009, p. 5). This panic is largely the result of traditional "effects" studies of media influence on young consumers. These studies, critiqued by Gauntlett (2008) for imposing deterministic and universalized conclusions and using simplistic, linear research designs, isolate a single media text (e.g., a song lyric) and conclude that it is harmful to all young people irrespective of contextual and individual factors. The second common response is a "kids will be kids" position, which dismisses youth's interests and critical capacity, while also depicting adults as uninterested, unengaged, and unaccountable in their relationships with youth. Neither of these is the whole story, or a particularly useful story, about youth, the adults in their lives, and their relationships with popular culture.

As a therapist, I must remain firm that "*not condemning something is not the same as endorsing it*" (Tilsen & Nylund, 2009, p. 5, italics in original). In order to invite individuals into conversations where they may think critically and consider new possibilities, I acknowledge both the problematic and productive potential of youth's engagement with popular culture. Social construction, queer theory, and cultural studies provide a conceptual footing and a relational positioning that allow for the contradictions, complexities, and possibilities posed by queer youth's engagement with popular culture. I encourage my clients to break binaries, not TVs.

FOR REFLECTION

- *How have you thought about youth's consumption of popular culture?*
- *In what ways do you engage with youth around their interest in pop culture? Does this change when you are talking to a youth who is a client?*
- *Would you say that you have: (1) not considered engaging with youth around popular culture at all, (2) seen talking about it only as way to join with them, or (3) understood it as a significant and meaningful aspect of identity and a rich resource for therapeutic conversations?*
- *What has your professional training taught you about leveraging popular culture in therapy? What do you make of that?*
- *Which analysis do you tend to organize around —that the culture industries hold unchallenged power over consumers or that consumers have interpretive agency? Why?*
- *Imagine a conversation with a youth informed by the premise that he or she is a passive consumer of popular culture. Now imagine a conversation informed by the idea that youth interpret and shape the meanings of the popular culture texts they interact with. How do you change your positioning within the relationship? How might the conversations go in each instance?*

MORE THAN A TRANSITIONAL OBJECT— IDENTITY IN A BAG: A CASE CONSULTATION

In the professional training video *Therapy as Social Construction* (McNamee & Tilsen, 2011), Sheila McNamee consults a therapist, Jeff, about a case where he feels stuck. Jeff discusses his work with a fourteen-year-old who is transitioning from male to female. Jeff describes the family as being fully understanding and supportive of Eric's[7] transition. In fact, she was receiving hormone therapy to deter the effects of puberty, a common medical practice in support of transitioning youth.

Eric had been diagnosed with Asperger's disorder by another clinician involved in her care. Managing the behaviors associated with the Asperger's diagnosis was Eric's parents' primary concern, as they saw Eric's struggles in social situations and relationships as problematic for both Eric and the family. As is common with people labeled as such, Eric often was enthusiastically and nearly exclusively focused on and fascinated by one thing. Eric's one thing was a Gucci bag—she wanted it desperately.

As Jeff initially describes his work with Eric, he conveys his concern with Eric's dedicated interest in obtaining a Gucci bag and how that would become a focus of their conversations. This focus seemed to come at the expense of other issues that Jeff thought to be more central and substantive to Eric and her family: taunting at school, a power struggle with her parents about her preference for homeschooling, interpersonal difficulties, and a lack of situational awareness. Jeff acknowledges his inclination to view the Gucci bag as "materialistic" and as something of a distraction from addressing the significant challenges facing Eric and her family. He notes that Eric acknowledged struggling with worries about how she was treated at school; however, sustaining a goal-oriented conversation about this had eluded Jeff. Jeff sighs and says, "I can't get her to talk about anything else but the Gucci bag. . . ."

After listening to Jeff for a while, Sheila gently begins to ask questions that invite him to reconsider the possible importance of focusing on Eric's overall experience of gender and transition. She invites Jeff to reconsider the significance of the Gucci bag:

> *Sheila:* Eric's desire to talk about things that seem not to matter—wanting to buy things—given all that she's confronting . . . I'm wondering if she may be offering those conversations as a way to engage in her comfortable identity. And the conversation with you is a comfortable place to do that. What do you think would happen if you would embrace what you think is a materialistic conversation as a way to get into the conversation that you've been asked to have?

Sheila suggests that, rather than understand the Gucci bag to be a "throw-away line, a side story" distracting from the "real stuff of Asperger's," that the Gucci bag is brimming with meaning and significance. Participating in a Gucci bag conversation is not merely a joining strategy. Sheila explicitly invites Jeff to consider "creating a story around the Gucci bag that's about identity and transition," and she points out that a Gucci bag "is an icon of a very feminine identity." Sheila thus integrates a constructionist ethos and a cultural studies sensibility—and leaves lots of room for queering the yet-to-be-spoken story of Eric's identity.

She suggests to Jeff that it is possible to find a preferred construction of identity (and a story that sustains it) within what the client offers and finds meaningful. She also suggests that Jeff reengage with *what Eric brings up* in a way that allows Eric to identify the significance for herself from her position as a young transwoman, rather than from Jeff's position as an adult who questions consumer consumption and as a therapist who sees other problems to address. Further, she makes use of the cultural studies notion that youth's relationships with popular culture artifacts are imbued with meaning and that, through a process of engaged inquiry, they can make meaning about (and from) their relationships with pop culture.

Finally, in Jeff's work with Eric, there exists a great deal of potential for queering dominant understandings of gender and Gucci bags (among other things). The prevailing understandings available to us about Gucci bags are located within discourses of consumerism and traditional versions of hyper-femininity; thus, we may readily dismiss a teenager's interest in such things as the machinations of American adolescence. However, the idea of a *fourteen-year-old transgender female* rocking a Gucci bag disrupts these understandings as they intersect with the discourses of the gender binary, heteronormativity, and potentially, social class. This provides an opening for a conversation between Jeff and Eric about the meanings Eric makes regarding her desire for a Gucci bag and her transition to her preferred identity. Jeff acknowledges to Sheila that the significance of Eric's identity (and the bag as an icon of identity) "wasn't on my radar," and he expresses interest in pursuing the possibility of such a conversation with Eric.

Elsewhere in the video, Jeff notes that he and Eric had discussed another aspect of popular culture, the TV show *RuPaul's Drag Race.*[8] Demonstrating great creativity (as well as the subversion of some traditional notions of clinical practice and intervention), Jeff had suggested that Eric write a letter to the first winner of the show, BeBe. Eric had been particularly interested in Bebe, in part because she had lived in Eric's hometown. Jeff's suggestion, anchored in the narrative therapy practice of creating supportive and appreciative audiences, was intended to help her identify and reach out to potential allies. Interestingly, until his consultation with Sheila, Jeff did not consider how his idea of connecting Eric with BeBe was about identity.

Sheila's consultation in this video also included the presence of a reflecting team.[9] These three senior clinicians positioned themselves as witnesses to the consultative conversation and offered their reflections. The significance of the Gucci bag was not lost on the team. As one member noted, "I think as adults we tend to discount the things that kids are into and what they attach value to. Here's something Eric is really into and there's some identity attached to the Gucci bag and some meaning to be made. As therapists we need permission to talk to kids about things that might seem shallow but that hold tons of meaning to them."

We therapists often feel that we lack permission from the discourses that define the professional practice of therapy to engage with the idea that something meaningful can be found—*or made*—out of youth's relationship with popular culture. I would take this one step further: what is implicit in this lack of permission is a lack of conceptual maps that *legitimate* a purposeful interest in popular culture as a line of therapeutic inquiry, as well as a lack of conversational resources for engaging meaningfully with youth about their relationships with pop culture. A therapeutic practice informed by a cultural studies perspective, however, provides those maps, resources, and legitimacy.

REFLECTIONS ON CHAPTER 6

BY SARAH DACK AND COURTNEY SLOBOGIAN

We can agree that it could be an important therapeutic practice to critically think about pop culture in relation to queer youth identity construction. We appreciate the articulation of the dialectical relationship between media and audience as a way of giving agency to queer youth as consumers of pop culture.

One of the things we've held on to after reading this chapter is the way that in Western media and society, the body has come to stand in as somewhat of a surrogate for certain aspects of identity, as described by Julie in the introduction to this chapter. The idea that consumption of media/products can come to represent identity and queerness creates space for intention. Once we recognize that our bodies are being seen as a site of representation for certain aspects of our identity, we can take control of that representation and begin to consciously shape it in ways that resist hegemonic norms. This process of using our bodies to queer media representation will be an ongoing endeavor as media continues to be informed by the ways we attempt to queer it; it's a completely dialectical relationship, one in which we maintain the ability to resist norms and shape representation.

Participating in this work has helped us to realize that to a certain degree our "critical lenses" are intensely steeped in academia. What this means is that we have to work at pulling things apart in a different way. In a sense, we're working our way back from the center. We're constantly working at seeing the value in popular media themes outside of that theoretical lens because we can take it to a certain point where it's impossible to enjoy consuming pop culture. There is a space to inhabit where our critical lens still allows us to access pop culture in a manageable way. We have both started to move in a direction where we are becoming more able to engage with pop culture in an enjoyable way without feeling like we are necessarily compromising our critical understandings of it. Nothing articulates this point more clearly than the fact that we have both recently opened Twitter accounts so as to be able to follow Justin Bieber. This activity was propelled by the discovery of a blog entitled *Lesbians Who Look Like Justin Bieber*. This example articulates the experience of finding ways to navigate things as they are and being able to find pleasure in them without constantly feeling the need to defend or resist as though our lives (identities?) depended upon it.

Having the awareness that there is an expectation that our engagement and involvement in pop culture does say something to those around us about our identities means that we're never quite able to completely enjoy something without considering how it contributes to the construction of our identity. Despite the fact that we look like excited fourteen-year-olds when we spot Justin Bieber on the front of a *People* magazine in Safeway, we can still explain to you the radical notion of being interested in a sixteen-year-old pop singer who embodies some sort of queer female sensibility . . . whether he intends it or not.

NOTES

1. Excellent critical applications toward this end include: Battles and Hilton-Morrow (2002); Manuel (2009); and Westerfelhaus and Lacroix (2006). Gauntlett's (2008) *Media, Gender & Identity* and his website (theory.org.uk) provide helpful and accessible introductions to the study of media and identity.
2. The notion of vertical and horizontal culture was introduced by Maalouf (2000).
3. In cultural studies, *text* refers to anything that produces meaning.
4. "Textual poaching" is an active reading of mass media texts. By inserting oneself into the text, consumers engage in individual and fluid interpretation. This practice invites subversive interpretations and opens space for counterhegemonic practices (although all alternative readings are not automatically transgressive of or resistant to dominant ideologies).
5. Dobby was the elf-servant of the Malfoy family in Harry Potter. A common reading of the elves in the stories is that they represent the economic underclass.
6. For further examples of therapists exploring clients' relationships with pop culture, see: Boucher (2003), Nylund (2007), Rubin (2008), Sullivan (2008), Tilsen and Nylund (2009, 2012).
7. Jeff explained that "Eric" (a pseudonym Jeff used in consultation) was at the time of the consultation using female pronouns and the boy name given her by her parents. She had yet to settle on a girl name.
8. *RuPaul's Drag Race* is a reality TV show on the Logo network in the United States. RuPaul, a famous and iconic drag queen, hosts the show, on which hopefuls compete to be the next superstar drag queen.
9. For more about reflecting teams, see Anderson (1991); Friedman (1995); and White (1995). In this video, Sheila discusses the use and purpose of the reflecting team.

Chapter Seven

Bullies, Bible-Bangers, and Haters

When Others Don't Want It to Get Better

Homosexuals are barbarians that need to be disciplined and educated.

—Marcus Bachman, psychotherapist[1]

I went to see this therapist. I told him how I felt and he just pretty much dismissed me, told me there's no such thing as trans and that I was crazy.

—Mateo, Q-Squad member

From the daily microaggressive epithets that pick away at the soul to murder by homo- and transphobia,[2] the tragic truth is that many queer youth live in risky circumstances. These material realities are not, as some may suggest, arguments *against* the notion that we live in a socially constructed, discursively produced world. On the contrary, queer youth's experiences of harassment, drug use, homelessness, poverty, school absence, pregnancy, and death demonstrate all too well the power of discourse.

It is a gross and irresponsible error to think that social construction means that "nothing is real" or that everything is *just* stories. It should be clear by now that social construction is a process of creating lived experiences that have very material effects. Some effects benefit certain people at the expense of others. Stories do matter. We need to construct them thoughtfully—and with justice in mind.

AGE MATTERS

In chapter 3, I reviewed the history of the contemporary gay rights movement in the United States, with an emphasis on the discursive production of identity categories. The original gay rights movement focused on basic civil and human rights, including freedom from police harassment and brutality. Subsequent priorities over the last forty years have been equal access in housing and employment, marriage equality and related domestic rights, parental and adoption rights, and open participation in the military. Thus, the overwhelming concern of this movement has been with *adult* rights. The primary focus on young people has been in the context of demanding parental rights for LGBT parents to adopt or keep their kids, and on the stabilizing effects that the legalization of same-sex marriage will have on the children of LGBT parents.

In the last several years, as youth have come out in greater numbers and at earlier ages, and as more youth take up LGBT and queer identities, social awareness of the existence of queer and LGBT youth has grown. However, this awareness has emerged to a large extent because of the threats youth face.

The contemporary gay rights movement emerged during a cultural moment when the idea of homosexual (let alone queer) youth didn't exist. To be sure, hate crime laws and nondiscrimination laws benefit people of all ages, and help produce a discourse of inclusion that values everyone. They fail, however, to account for the unique and immediate needs of young people—particularly those experiencing risk. Overwhelmingly, these needs are basic: adequate housing, youth-centered health care, safe educational environments, sexual and chemical health education and resources, supportive and active adults in their lives, and culturally responsive emergency services. Because young people can't vote and aren't income earners, it is incumbent on adults to champion their needs.

Unlike other marginalized groups, where youth share the same social locations as their parents and other family and community members, queer youth are likely to be alone in their queerness within their family. Thus, many cannot rely on their parents, families, or religious and ethnic communities to protect and care for them. Sadly, it is often in these contexts, where other young people gain support and protection, that queer youth experience violence to their psyches and their bodies. Religious discourses are especially pernicious, inciting much consternation, confusion, and self-hatred for young queers and driving wedges between parents and children.

As for schools, the extent to which queer youth are safely included and supported varies. School climates typically reflect the social and political climates of the communities they serve. As a result, the school experiences of youth are extremely varied and depend in part on the breadth of school anti-harassment policies and the robustness with which they are enforced, the existence of Gay Straight Alliances, LGBT-focused student support services, and curriculum that addresses LGBT history and sexual education.

Consider these statistics:[3]

- 60 percent of LGBT students report feeling unsafe at school.
- Almost 50 percent of transgender students report skipping class at least once and missing at least one day of school in the past month because they felt unsafe or uncomfortable.
- 90 percent of LGBT students report being harassed or assaulted at school.
- 25 percent of transgender youth attempt suicide.
- LGB youth are up to four times more likely to attempt suicide than straight youth.
- Nearly two times as many LGBT youth use drugs and alcohol as straight youth.
- 20 to 40 percent of all homeless youth identify as LGBT.
- 62 percent of homeless LGB youth will attempt suicide at least once—more than two times as many as their heterosexual peers.
- LGB youth from highly rejecting families are more than eight times as likely to have attempted suicide than those who report low levels of family rejection.
- Only 18 percent of schools with bully-prevention programs address LGBT issues.

These statistics reveal how unsafe queer youth are, especially in the two places that should afford them the greatest security: home and school. In the face of such numbers, what's a therapist to do?

This book has provided you with some conceptual and conversational resources to help you position yourself in ways that are supportive and responsive to youth—even when they are facing dire circumstances or enduring trauma.

When our clients face particularly difficult or tragic situations, we therapists can forget what we know about positioning and relationships, about our skills and our clients' skills, about deconstructing limiting and specifying discourses, about making meaning and being curious. Our attention can be captured by the difficult situation. We may then fail to leverage all the resources that exist between our clients and us. At these times, we need to step back and remember what we know.

In particular, we can remind ourselves to situate problems within the discourses that produce them. By contextually locating problems such as suicide, homelessness, violence, and drug use, we deprivatize those problems. We also challenge the prevailing cultural practice of burdening individuals and, more accurately, place accountability on oppressive cultural practices and institutions.

For example, consider suicide. The prevailing discourses encourage us to go to medicalized accounts of psychopathology. By definition, these are individualized accounts of identity. These accounts include assessments levied against a person, such as "depressed," "hopeless," "helpless," and "angry." We may often wish that this individual had done something differently—that they would have "reached out," "asked for help," "left their situation," "been, stronger," or "taken their meds."

However, when we take a constructionist stance that people exist in relationships, both with other people and with influential cultural discourses, we become curious about the implied *individual* act of killing oneself. We may ask, for example:

- *What conditions would lead someone to feel so depressed and hopeless?*
- *Who or what is responsible for these conditions?*
- *How does the degree of helplessness they may have felt reflect the extent of the challenges they faced?*
- *Who or what is responsible for the challenges this person may have faced?*
- *Who benefits from the conditions that created these challenges?*
- *Why do we ask why the person did not reach out? What would it mean to ask why no one apparently reached in?*
- *How much stronger should they have been? Are there limits to our individual capacity to outpower some things?*
- *If we consider that this person was murdered, who or what would be the prime suspects? Who or what would be accessories or coconspirators?*
- *How might people respond differently if we considered this murder by transphobia, that is, committed by discourses deployed by the gender binary and hetero- and homonormativity?*

This is a process of *diagnosing discourses,* not people. Here is a practice that can help you build your skills in diagnosing discourses:

1. List the common risks and traumas faced by queer youth. For example, physical and sexual violence, bullying, homelessness, spiritual abuse, drug use, suicide, etc.
2. Identify and list the individualized and pathologizing accounts, labels, and assessments that locate each problem within individual queer youth. Describe the symptoms that an individual youth may experience that support these accounts. For example, a youth may skip school, seem sullen and anxious, and report headaches. From an individualized perspective, the youth may be assessed to have an anxiety disorder and suffer from "low self-esteem" and "lack of motivation."
3. Now, from a constructionist perspective, relabel and offer contextualized accounts that understand this youth's relationship to each problem in context. For example, instead of diagnosing the youth with an anxiety disorder, consider the youth's experience within the context of a hostile and unwelcoming school climate. Skipping school may be

understood as a self-protection strategy; feeling anxious is a sensible response to cruel treatment, one that keeps him or her vigilant. Instead of locating "lack of motivation" inside the youth, we can wonder about a context that is less than motivating, one that fails to engage the youth around what matters to him or her.

4. Finally, make up a diagnosis[4] of the discourse. For example, in the case of murder by transphobia: "Gender Inflexibility Disorder, Transphobic Features, Patriarchal Violence Subtype." Or, in the example above, "HSGB Anxiety Disorder" (Homophobic School Gender Binary Anxiety Disorder).

As therapists, we can borrow the realtor's mantra, "location, location, location," to remember how important it is to tend to the social location of problems and to situate them within discourse. In doing this, we can help youth be liberated from the ideas that the oppression they experience is their fault, that they deserve it, and that there is something wrong with them. This experience then makes room for them to create other identity conclusions.

But what about the hopelessness that can ensue even when we understand violence and other traumatic conditions in context? Some people suggest it is just as disheartening (perhaps even more so) to take stock of an oppressive, pervasive discourse. Our work doesn't end with locating the problem within discourse. Our conversations with clients also bring forward people's acts of resistance to these prevailing discourses. These conversations invite the consideration of alternative discourses that support the emergence of preferred identities. They also deprivatize problems, de-isolate individuals through remembering practices, and encourage multiple perspectives in support of queer youth identity performances. This process places queer youth (and those who support them) in *resistance* to oppressive or hegemonic discourses, and encourages them to relocate their preferred stories, and alternative versions of themselves, within discourses that support them.

FROM THERAPIST TO ACTIVIST: OUT OF YOUR OFFICE AND INTO THE STREETS

Therapy is a political act.

—Marcia Hill, feminist therapist scholar

Our job is to change the world in fifty-minute increments.

—Ken Hardy, family therapy scholar

Our work does not stop when we leave our consulting rooms. Indeed, how can we promote a discursive, relational, deprivatized practice informed by queer theory if we keep it sequestered away within the confines of a very private practice? If we understand problems to be socially located and that discourse shapes and gives meaning to personal narratives, is it possible *or ethical* to only work on the micro level with clients? Especially when we take up issues of youth safety, education, murder, and suicide, is it possible to think our work is done after the fifty-minute hour?

Social construction suggests that we constantly consider broader contexts in which to act. Queer theory insists that we disrupt conventional notions of what constitutes "professional practice," and that we deprivatize therapy by enlarging our focus to cultural and systemic change. To that end, I suggest the following practices, which can extend your reach and have a real impact in the world.

1. *Know the political climate you live in.* What are the state, local, and school laws and regulations that impact queer youth and their families? Keep up with changes in these laws and regulations. Understand the living circumstances of the youth you work with and how the relevant laws impact them.
2. *Know about queer-youth-friendly resources and how to access them.* Be able to make a *good* referral. A good referral means you have personal knowledge about the agency *and* the person you are referring a client to. This means you will need to take some field trips to meet others, participate in local conferences and community projects, and serve on committees that support queer youth. Also, keep track of what queer youth say about different services and professionals. For example, some agencies and programs may be fine for adults, but don't make youth feel welcome.
3. *Be connected to the youth work community.* Get to know some of the frontline, in-the-streets programs and staff members so that you have a direct pipeline to resources and programs that queer youth may need. These include: health care, birth control, safer sex information and STI/HIV testing, housing and emergency shelter, legal advocacy, drop-in youth spaces, walk-in counseling, access to food and bus vouchers, and arts and recreation opportunities.
4. *Build relationships with school staff who are allies.* Be selective and informed about who you send youth to for school support. Keep your contacts up to date. This is particularly important if a school does not have LGBT-inclusive policies and programs.
5. *Know something about different cultures and religions and have some queer-youth-friendly connections in various communities.* For queer youth from some religious and cultural communities, it may be very difficult to find adults and community places that provide safety and a welcoming climate. Find cultural consultants to help you understand these communities and create connections that support queer youth.

Learn which church and other religious organizations in your area are queer inclusive so you can provide a good referral for a youth looking for someone from the same religious tradition.

6. *Keep PFLAG*[5] *and other relevant and local information handy in your office.* Provide support for family members of the queer youth you serve.
7. *Know about and participate in the important LGBT and queer events in your community, such as Pride celebrations and Transgender Day of Remembrance.* It's important to fold yourself into the community and knowledgably support youth's participation in these events.
8. *Be political.* Vote. Pay attention to what impacts youth. It's not about single-issue voting or LGBT issues alone. It's about school safety, economic justice, accessible housing, youth-centered and affordable health care, sexual and chemical health education, arts education, reproductive rights, youth services, and so on. Work to educate politicians and policy makers about the real life impact of their decisions on queer youth. Thank them when they get something right.
9. *Be an activist.* Work to change the systems that perpetuate oppression. Act in solidarity with queer youth by embracing the notion that *your struggle is my struggle*.

NOTES

1. Marcus Bachman is an unlicensed psychotherapist in suburban Minnesota who practices conversion therapy.

2. I consider it to be murder, not suicide, when queer youth kill themselves. Labeling it as suicide participates in the privatizing of social problems, perpetuates individualizing highly contextual actions, and obscures damaging discourses and those who incite them. Similarly, I reject the all-too-frequent social service moniker of "at-risk youth" for the same reasons.

3. Data from GLSEN's 2009 school climate survey, available at www.glsen.org/cgi-bin/iowa/all/research/index.html, and from The Trevor Project website, available at www.thetrevorproject.org.

4. A reminder: DSM diagnoses are socially constructed! For more on the social construction of disorder, see McNamee (2002).

5. Parents, families, and friends of lesbians and gays, www.pflag.org.

Chapter Eight

Resisting Conclusions

> *If a therapist is really invested in their identity as a lesbian woman and they're listening to someone talk about being queer . . . I feel like that's where they have to be good at what they do or they could really fuck someone up. . . . They could be equally invested in the categories gay, lesbian, bisexual, transgender as a straight person just because it would be easy for them to understand.*
>
> —Sarah, Q-Squad member

I began this book project resolute in my position that I did not intend to write yet another how-to therapy manual. Indeed, this book is a polemic against such an exercise of certainty. I did want to write about the *doing of* responsive, respectful work with queer youth. Thus, I have tried to maintain the distinction between rendering universal, static, expert edicts and providing resources for a supple practice that stays in constant motion, and reflects the fluid lives of queer youth. This position was confirmed and fortified through my conversations with Sarah, Dylan, Ruben, Mateo, and Courtney. Time and time again they reminded me, explicitly or implicitly, that not only are the maps of their identities not yet drawn up, but the territories are often yet to be created. When a territory *is* created, it is likely to look quite different from youth to youth. Even then, the map has been written in pencil, and is likely to shift and change.

My clinical work with queer youth and their families has confirmed for me the need to keep space open for all sorts of developments. As long as I stay close to the experiences of those I consult, and cast a critical eye toward the products of modern psychology that pass as universal truths (e.g., models of identity development, prescriptive stages for coming out, treatment strategies and techniques, insistence on a stable constitution of self), I will have the opportunity to witness and participate in the creation of meaningful possibilities.

Indeed, if there is one thing that shouts out from of the 150-plus pages of Q-Squad transcripts and my scores of hours in therapeutic conversations with queer youth, it's that there are no "right" answers, no definitive conclusions to be drawn.

But that doesn't mean it's not possible to get it wrong. Every member of the Q-Squad had a story to tell of someone—a clinician, family member, friend, acquaintance, or lover—who made incorrect assumptions, insisted that they were something they were not, or ignored a critical dimension of identity. My young clients tell me stories of being misread, misunderstood, mistaken, and otherwise misserved by previous therapists. These acts, from annoying imposition to spiritual violence, were committed by people irrespective of their gender or sexual identity.

We all experience assumptions being made about us and aspects of our identities going ignored. When working with queer youth, it is important to acknowledge—both to them and to ourselves—that they walk in a discursive world of wrong assumptions and blind disregard. How can we minimize the chance of doing wrong without trying to be right? One possibility can be found in the relationship of the two discursive frames expounded in these pages: insider knowledges and academic literacies. This book is an articulation of how I operationalize the relationship between these two frames. Two questions guided me: *How do queer youth live the ideas articulated in queer theory? In what ways is queer theory brought to life and made more real and accessible by their lives?* Throughout my conversations with the Q-Squad members, I took note of the recursive and productive relationship between queer theory and their lived experiences. An ongoing awareness of this relationship in our practice can guide us away from wrong and right and toward the productive generation of meaning. Conversations that amplify this relationship and that are curiosity driven rather than certainty driven help us avoid limitations and declarations of certitude.

In this generative, liminal, and potentially meaningful space created and re-created between lived experience and theory, we therapists can make critical decisions about how to relate with queer youth.

By engaging reflectively with both theory and lived experiences (ours and our clients'), we move toward Freire's (1999) notion of *praxis*—action and reflection for the purpose of transforming the world. Moving from talk to action is a critical aspect of praxis and crucial to the larger project of social justice. This involves constant personal reflection in an effort to deconstruct discourses and examine what influences our ideas and informs our actions. It also involves asking questions of clients that allow them to do the same. This process of reflection informs what we *do*—how and what we talk about, and what actions come from this talk.

For example, we may ask ourselves the reflective questions that appear throughout this book, as well as other questions that emerge from our work.

Our answers to these questions can influence the choices we make in practice, thus taking us from talk to action.

When I first began asking myself questions about my early understandings of gender, I became more and more aware of how the assumptions I made in therapy reflected the dominance of the gender binary. As I continued to reflect on the consequences of this, I realized that these assumptions were incompatible with my preference for privileging clients' meanings and with my ethics of relational engagement and justice. Over time, I am better at deconstructing my assumptions and moving beyond them. Through reflection to action, I am transforming my practice. I say *transforming* (rather than *transformed*), because praxis is always a process.

For further inspiration to blaze the trail of praxis, we need look no further than the Q-Squad. In the final meeting of the Q-Squad, members identified not only ways in which they were thinking and talking about things differently, but also ways in which these differences shaped their actions in their interpersonal relationships and communities. Below are excerpts from this conversation:

> *Ruben:* I want to say that the talking about this stuff has been really great and really fulfilling. It's really sad that it's our last gathering. Mateo and I are actually working on releasing an art-heavy queer culture 'zine for Winnipeg's queer community.
>
> *Julie:* Cool! I'm wondering: What things from these conversations and your experience here, Ruben, may be something you see as contributing to this project, or maybe something you might want to carry forward to your 'zine?
>
> *Ruben*: I don't think we would've created a queer, art-heavy 'zine. Whenever I would leave one of these meetings I'd feel really fulfilled and my creative juices were flowing and I'd go write things down. This will be great for the project.
>
> *Julie:* What are some other ways people feel like they'll be taking this with them, or what would you like to come from this experience?
>
> *Dylan*: Now when I come across someone who feels like they aren't so sure where their sexual orientation may be leaning toward, I like to give them ideas or explain a little about queer theory so that they can have an idea of what's out there . . . I think for me I've become more inquisitive of people.

> *Sarah*: I feel like for me something I'm going to take away . . . knowing that it makes a difference to intentionally create space to hear other people's opinions and not assume.

Central to this reflexivity and mutuality is humility. By this I don't mean shame, timidity, or self-abasement; but a lack of pretense and an awareness that I know no more than others. Humility allows me to let my clients bring their knowledge to our conversations. It keeps me out of the way, yet it doesn't remove me from the process. Without humility, I would not be able to engage in the practices discussed throughout this work: asking questions from a position of curiosity, avoiding assessment or judgment, being able to be surprised.

As my work with the Q-Squad unfolded, my humility grew as I experienced the uncommon wisdom of the team. At times, I struggled to keep humility close as I flirted with ideas of controlling the process more. When this happened, the conversation tended to be less generative and engaging. A lesson in humility to be sure, and one I remind myself of every time I am with a client.[1]

FOR REFLECTION

Take some time to reflect on where you started, where you are now, and where you could be headed in relationship to the ideas presented in this book. Ask yourself these questions:

- *Think about your understandings of social construction and queer theory, and your ideas about working with queer youth. What has stayed the same and what has changed for you since reading this book?*
- *What are some new ways that you see social construction and queer theory as resources for your practice?*
- *As you go forward, how would you like these ideas to inform your work with queer youth? What will you be doing differently because of these ideas?*
- *What questions have been answered for you in this book? What questions remain unanswered? What new questions have emerged?*
- *How would you describe yourself as a therapist now? In what ways has this description stayed the same since reading this book? How has it changed?*
- *In what areas of your life outside your practice have the ideas in this book influenced you?*
- *What are your ideas about how you can practice with humility? What are your ideas about how you can practice in ways that are responsive and fluid?*

- *How do you avoid the right/wrong binary? How do you engage in praxis?*
- *What else stands out for you that you want to remember and carry forward?*

STILL MORE QUESTIONS

I ended the Q-Squad meetings because I needed to put a wrap on the inquiry process and start writing, not because we were tired of meeting or found ourselves staring at our toes with nothing to say. Indeed, there continued to be much energy and interest in talking. The team members experienced the talking as both generative and invigorating, with each conversation inspiring the desire for more.

I asked the Q-Squad what things they thought professionals should think about. Below are excerpts from our final meeting where we discussed this topic.

> *Sarah:* . . . having you talk about ways of being a therapist that can be queer in ways that are outside of traditional practitioner style seemed super important and interesting. Like when you asked us, "What are some ways you think that therapists could approach working with queer youth that could be respectful, important, useful, and meaningful?" That feels like a really hopeful conversation to have.
>
> *Julie*: Are you suggesting more conversations where queer youth can serve as advisors?
>
> *Sarah:* Yeah, because that to me seems like such a good way of doing things. . . . Because I think that specifically with therapy, people have shitty experiences, and you're like, "Well, that was a fucking shitty experience" and you don't do anything with it. To actually have something done with your shitty fucking experience is helpful. To know that there are ways of doing productive things with your shitty experiences that could potentially change the experiences of other people, I think that's really important. And really important for me to know that that could make someone rethink the way that they talk to youth, that's pretty important.

Yes, indeed. That is what compelled me to write this book: the idea that we ought to rethink the way that we talk to, with, and about youth, especially queer youth. This rethinking begins with a repositioning that places youth as advisors to the process.

Sarah's comments—endorsed and repeated by the members of the Q-Squad over the course of three months, six gatherings, and ten hours of discussion, and frequently echoed in my therapeutic conversations with other youth—would suggest that to do anything else would be an enormous failure to listen, reflect, and respond in just and ethical ways. It is my hope that you join me in their hope that they will be taken seriously.

NOTE

1. Interestingly, one criticism of the embrace of humility as a virtue comes from Nietzsche, who saw humility as a weakness in part because it was incompatible with his privileging of individualism.

Appendix

Sex-Positive Resources

WEBSITES

Advocates for Youth: www.advocatesforyouth.org

A national advocacy organization that promotes comprehensive sex education. Information for parents and professionals.

Answer: www.answer.rutgers.edu

Run by Rutgers University. This is a resource for adults, both professionals and parents. It provides online training and much information about sex education.

Midwest Teen Sex Show: www.midwestteensexshow.com

A sexual health website that uses short video podcasts to provide information on sex for teens and young adults. Very engaging and funny, but also provides excellent information.

Planned Parenthood for Teens: www.plannedparenthood.org/info-for-teens/

This site provides straightforward health information.

Scarleteen: www.scarleteen.com

A comprehensive sexual health website for teens. Much of the content is youth created.

Sex, etc.: www.sexetc.org

Sex education magazine and website by and for teens. Run by Rutgers University.

BOOKS

Corinna, H. (2007). *S.E.X.: The all-you-need-to-know progressive sexuality guide to get you through high school and college.* New York: Marlowe & Company.

This book provides comprehensive coverage of sexual health, bodies, body image, healthy relationships, sexual pleasure, gender and sexual identity.

Roffman, D. M. (2001). *Sex and sensibility: The thinking parent's guide to talking sense about sex.* Cambridge, MA: Perseus Publishing.

This book is a practical resource for adults who want to have effective conversations with young people about sex.

Schalet, A. T. (2011). *Not under my roof: Parents, teens and the culture of sex.* Chicago: University of Chicago Press.

This book provides a cultural analysis of American attitudes about youth sexuality by contrasting it to Dutch culture. It includes a discussion of ways to shift from the emphasis on sex as a risk to a focus on self-control and responsibility.

References

Abbott, S., & Love, B. (1973). *Sappho was a right-on woman: A liberated view of lesbianism.* New York: Stein & Day.

Adorno, T. W. (1991). *The culture industry: Selected essays on mass culture.* London: Routledge.

Alinder, G. (1992). Gay liberation meets the shrinks. In Jay & Young (Eds.), *Out of the closets* (pp. 141–144). New York: New York University Press.

Andersen, T. (1991). *The reflecting team: Dialogues and dialogues about the dialogues.* New York: Norton.

Ang, A. (1996). *Living room wars: Rethinking media audiences for a postmodern world.* New York: Routledge.

American Psychiatric Association. (2000). *Diagnostic and statistical manual of mental disorders,* Fourth Edition, Text Revision. Washington, DC: American Psychiatric Association.

Anderson, H., & Burney, J. P. (2004). A postmodern collaborative approach: A family's reflections on "in-the-room" and "on-the-challenge course" therapy: It's all language. In T. Strong & D. Pare (Eds.), *Furthering talk: Advances in discursive therapies* (pp. 87–108). New York: Kluwer Academic Press.

Bakhtin, M. M. (1986). *Speech genres and other late essays.* Austin: University of Texas Press.

Barker, C. (2000). *Cultural studies: Theory and practice.* Thousand Oaks, CA: Sage.

Battles, K., & Hilton-Morrow, W. (2002). Gay characters in conventional spaces: Will and Grace and the situation comedy genre. *Critical Studies in Media Communication, 19*(1), 87–105.

Bell, S., & Pepper, R. (2008). *The transgender child: A handbook for families and professionals.* San Francisco: Cleis Press.

Berger, P., & Luckmann, T. (1966). *The social construction of reality: A treatise in the sociology of knowledge.* New York: Doubleday.

Billig, M. (1990). Collective memory, ideology and the British royal family. In D. Middleton & D. Edwards (Eds.), *Collective remembering.* London: Sage.

Bird, J. (2000). *The heart's narrative: Therapy and navigating life's contradictions.* Auckland: Edge Press.

Bohan, J. S., Russell, G. M., Cass, V., Haldeman, D. C., Iasenza, S., Klein, F., Omoto, M., & Tiefer, L. (1999). *Conversations about psychology and sexual orientation.* New York: New York Univesity Press.

Boucher, M. (2003). Exploring the meaning of tattoos. *International Journal of Narrative Therapy and Community Practice, 3,* 57–59.

Butler, C., & Byrne, A. (2008). Queer in practice: Therapy and queer theory. In L. Moon (Ed.), *Feeling queer or queer feelings?* (pp. 89–105). London: Routledge.

Butler, J. (1990a). *Gender trouble: Feminism and the subversion of identity*. New York: Routledge.

Butler, J. (1990b). Performative acts and gender constitution: An essay in phenomenology and feminist theory. In, S. E. Case (Ed.), *Performing feminisms: Feminist critical theory and theatre* (pp. 270–282). Baltimore: Johns Hopkins University Press.

Butler, J. (1993). *Bodies that matter: On the discursive limits of "sex."* New York: Routledge.

Butler, J. (1997). *Excitable speech: A politics of the performative*. New York: Routledge.

Butler, J. (2006). Undiagnosing gender. In P. Currah, R. M. Juang, & S. P. Minter (Eds.), *Transgender rights* (pp. 274–298). Minneapolis: University of Minnesota Press.

Cass, V. C. (1979). Homosexual identity formation: A theoretical model. *Journal of Homosexuality, 4*, 210–235.

Cass, V. C. (1984). Homosexual identity formation: Testing a theoretical model. *Journal of Sex Research, 20*(2), 143–167.

Chasin, A. (2000). *Selling out: The gay and lesbian movement goes to market*. New York: Palgrave.

Chiseri-Strater, E. (1991). *Academic literacies: The public and private discourses of university students*. Portsmouth, NH: Boynton.

Coleman, E. (1981/1982). Developmental stages of the coming out process. *Journal of Homosexuality, 7*(2–3), 31–43.

Crenshew, K. W. (1993). Beyond racism and misogyny: Black feminism and 2 Live Crew. In M. J. Matsuda, C. R. Lawrence, III, R. Delgado, & K. W. Crenshaw (Eds.), *Words that wound: Critical race theory, assaultive speech, and the first amendment* (pp. 111–132). Boulder: Westview Press.

Crimp, D. (1993). Right on, girlfriend! In M. Warner (Ed.), *Fear of a queer planet: Queer politics and social theory* (pp.300–320). Minneapolis: University of Minnesota Press.

Daly, M. (1973). *Beyond god the father: Toward a philosophy of women's liberation*. Boston: Beacon Press.

D'Augelli, A. R. (1994). Identity development and sexual orientation: Toward a model of lesbian, gay, and bisexual development. In E. J. Trickett, R. J. Watts, and D. Birman (Eds.), *Human diversity: Perspectives on people in context* (pp.312–333). San Francisco: Jossey-Bass.

D'Augelli, A. R., & Patterson, C. J. (Eds.). (2001). *Lesbian, gay, and bisexual identities and youth: Psychological perspectives*. New York: Oxford University Press.

Davies, B., & Harre, R. (1990). Positioning: The discursive production of selves. *Journal for the Theory of Social Behavior, 20*, 43–63.

de Lauretis, T. (1991). Queer theory: Lesbian and gay sexualities. *Differences: A Journal of Feminist Cultural Studies*, *3*(2), 296–313.

Derrida, J. (1967). *Of grammatology*. Baltimore: Johns Hopkins University Press.

Derrida, J. (1977). *Limited, Inc*. Evanston, IL: Northwestern University Press.

de Vries, G. (2008). Unsuitable for children. In, M. B. Sycamore (Ed.), *That's revolting! Queer strategies for resisting assimilation (rev.)* (pp. 141–146). Brooklyn: Soft Skull Press.

Doty, A. (1993). *Making things perfectly queer: Interpreting mass culture*. Minneapolis: University of Minnesota Press.

Duggan, L. (2002). *The incredible shrinking public: Sexual politics and the decline of democracy*. Boston: Beacon Press.

Ehrhardt, A. A. (1991). Preface. In E. Coleman (Ed.), *John Money: A tribute* (pp. xi–xvi). Binghamton, NY: Haworth Press.

Epston, D. (1993). Internalized other questioning with couples: The New Zealand version. In S. Gillian and R. Price (Eds.), *Therapeutic conversations* (pp. 183–189). New York: Norton.

Fish, L. S., & Harvey, R. G. (2005). *Nurturing queer youth: Family therapy transformed*. New York: Norton.

Fiske, J. (1989a). *Understanding popular culture*. London: Unwin Hyman.

Fiske, J. (1989b). *Reading the popular*. London: Unwin Hyman.

Forest, R., & Saewyc, E. M. (2004). Sexual minority teen parents: Demographics of an unexpected population. *Journal of Adolescent Health, 34*, 122.

Foucault, M. (1965). *Madness and civilization: A history of insanity in the age of reason*. New York: Random House. (Original work published in 1961.)
Foucault, M. (1970). *The order of things: An archeology of the human sciences*. New York: Pantheon (Original work published 1966).
Foucault, M. (1973). *Birth of the clinic: Archeaology of medical perception*. New York: Pantheon. (Original work published in 1963.)
Foucault, M. (1977). Truth and power. In C. Gordon (Ed.), *Power/knowledge: Selected interviews & other writings 1972–1977* (pp. 109–133). New York: Pantheon Books.
Foucault, M. (1978a). *The history of sexuality, Vol.1, An introduction*. New York: Pantheon. (Originally published in 1976.)
Foucault, M. (1978b). *Discipline and punish: The birth of the prison*. Middlesex: Peregrine Books. (Originally published in 1963.)
Foucault, M. (1982). The subject and power. In H. Dreyfus & P. Rabinow (Eds.), *Michel Foucault: Beyond structuralism and hermeneutics* (pp. 208–226). Chicago: University of Chicago Press.
Foucault, M. (1985). *The use of pleasure: The history of sexuality, Vol. 2*. New York: Pantheon. (Originally published in 1984.)
Foucault, M. (1988). Technologies of the self. In L. H. Martin, H. Gutman, & P. H. Hutton (Eds.), *Technologies of the self* (pp. 18–49). Amherst: University of Massachusetts Press.
Freire, P. (1999). *Pedagogy of the oppressed*. (3rd ed.) New York: Continuum.
Friedan, B. (1963). *The feminine mystique*. New York: Norton.
Friedman, S. (Ed.). (1995). *The reflecting team in action: Collaborative practices in family therapy*. New York: Guilford.
Garber, L. (2003). One step global, two steps back? Race, gender, and queer studies. *GLQ: A Journal of Lesbian and Gay Studies, 10*(1), 123–137.
Gauntlett, D. (2008). *Media, gender and identity: An introduction*. (2nd ed.). London: Routledge.
Geertz, C. (1973). Thick description: Toward an interpretive theory of cultures. In C. Geertz (Ed.), *The interpretation of cultures* (pp. 3–30). New York: Basic Books.
Gell, A. (2001). *The anthropology of time: Cultural constructions of temporal maps and images*. London: Berg Publishers.
Gergen, K. J. (1985). The social constructionist movement in modern psychology. *American Psychologist, 40* , 255–275.
Gergen, K. J. (1991). *The saturated self: Dilemmas of identity in contemporary life*. New York: Basic Books.
Gergen, K. J. (2009a). *An invitation to social construction* (2nd ed.). Sage: London.
Gergen, K. J. (2009b). *Relational being: Beyond self and community*. Oxford: Oxford University Press.
Gergen , M. (2003). Life stories: Pieces of a dream. In M. Gergen and K. J. Gergen (Eds.), *Social construction: A reader* (pp. 65–77). Los Angeles: Sage. (Originally published 1997.)
Gergen, M., & Gergen, K. J. (Eds.). (2003). *Social construction: A reader*. Los Angeles: Sage.
Glick, E. (2003). Introduction: Defining queer ethnicities. *GLQ: A Journal of Lesbian and Gay Studies, 10*(1), 123–124.
Gopinath, G. (2005). *Impossible desires: Queer diasporas and South Asian public cultures*. Durham: Duke University Press.
Guanaes, C., & Rasera, E. F. (2006). Therapy as social construction: An interview with Sheila McNamee. *Interamerican Journal of Psychology, 40*(1), 127–136.
Habermas, J. (1991). *The structural transformation of the public sphere: An inquiry into a category of bourgeois society*. Cambridge: MIT Press.
Halberstam, J. (1998). *Female masculinities*. Durham: Duke University Press.
Halberstam, J. (2005). *In a queer time and place: Transgender bodies, subcultural lives*. New York: New York University Press.
Hall, S. (1980). Cultural studies: Two paradigms. *Media, Culture, Society, 2*, 57–72.
Hall, S. (1997). Cultural identity and diaspora. In K. Woodward (Ed.), *Identity and difference* (pp. 51–59). London: Sage.

Halperin, D. M. (1997). *Saint Foucault: Towards a gay hagiography*. New York: Oxford University Press.

Hammonds, E. (1997). Black (w)holes and the geometry of black female sexuality. In E. Weed and N. Schor (Eds.), *Feminism meets queer theory* (pp.136–156). Bloomington: Indiana University Press.

Harré, R., & Van Langenhove, L. (Eds.) (1999). *Positioning theory: Moral contexts of intentional action*. Malden: Blackwell.

Hedtke, L. (2001a). Remembering practices in the face of death. *The Forum, 27*(2), 5–6.

Hedtke, L. (2001b). Stories of living and dying. *Gecko, 1*, 4–27.

Hedtke, L. (2003). The origami of re-membering. *International Journal of Narrative Therapy and Community work. 4,* 57–62.

Hedtke, L., & Winslade, J. (2004). *Re-membering lives: Conversations with the dying and bereaved*. Amityville, NY: Baywood Publishing.

Hodges, I. (2008). Queer dilemmas: The problem of power in psychotherapeutic and counseling practice. In L. Moon (Ed.), *Feeling queer or queer feelings?* (pp. 7–22). London: Routledge.

hooks, b. (1994). *Teaching to transgress: Education as the practice of freedom*. New York: Routledge.

Horkheimer, M., & Adorno, T. W. (2002). *Dialectic of enlightenment*. Palo Alto: Stanford University Press.

ICCE Manual Workgroup. (2012). *Feedback informed treatment and training manuals*. Chicago, IL: ICCE Press.

Jagose, A. (1996). *Queer theory: An introduction*. New York: NYU Press.

Jameson, F. (1991). *Postmodernism or, the cultural logic of late capitalism*. Durham: Duke University Press.

Jindal, P. (2008). Sites of resistance or sites of racism? In M. B. Sycamore (Ed.), *That's revolting! Queer strategies for resisting assimilation (rev.)* (pp. 39–46). Brooklyn: Soft Skull Press.

Katz, J. (1976). *Gay American history: Lesbians and gay men in the U.S.A*. New York: Thomas Cromwell.

Kellner, D. (1995). *Media culture: Cultural studies, identity, and politics between the modern and postmodern*. New York: Routledge.

Kuban, K., & Grinnell, C. (2008). More Abercrombie than activist? Queer working class rural youth vs. the new gay teenager. In, M. B. Sycamore (Ed.), *That's revolting! Queer strategies for resisting assimilation (rev.)* (pp. 78–86). Brooklyn: Soft Skull Press.

Langdridge, D. (2008). Are you angry or are you heterosexual? A queer critique of lesbian and gay models of identity development. In L. Moon (Ed.), *Feeling queer or queer feelings?* (pp. 23–35). London: Routledge.

Lesko, N. (2000). *Act your age! A cultural construction of adolescence*. New York: Routledge.

Levine, J. (2002). *Harmful to minors*. Minneapolis: University of Minnesota Press.

Lourde, A. (1980). *The cancer journals* (2nd ed.). San Francisco: Spinsters.

Maalouf, A. (2000). *On identity*. London: Routledge.

Madigan, S. (2008). Anticipating hope within writing and naming domains of despair. In C. Flaskas, I. McCarthy, & J. Sheehan (Eds.). *Hope and despair in narrative and family therapy: Adversity , forgiveness and reconciliation* (pp.100–112). New York: Bruner- Routledge.

Mallon, G. P. (2001). *Lesbian and gay youth issues*. Washington, DC: CWLA Press.

Mallon, G. P. (Ed.). (2009). *Social work practice with transgender and gender variant youth*. London: Routledge.

Manalansan IV, M. F. (2003). *Global divas: Filipino gay men in the diaspora*. Durham: Duke University Press.

Manuel, S. L. (2009). Becoming the homovoyeur: Consuming homosexual representation in queer as folk. *Social Semiotics, 19*(3), 275–291.

McNamee, S. (1996a). Out of the head and into the discourse: Therapeutic practice as relational engagement. *Dialogog Refleksjon, 35*. Norway: University of Tromso, pp. 118–130.

McNamee, S. (1996b). Therapy and identity construction in a postmodern world. In D. Gordin & T. R. Lindlof (Eds.), *Constructing the self in a mediated world* (pp. 141–155). London: Sage.

McNamee, S. (2000). The social poetics of relationally engaged research: Research as conversation. In K. Deissler & S. McNamee (Eds.), *Philosophy in therapy: The social poetics of therapeutic conversation* (pp.146–156). Heidelberg: Carl Auer Systeme Verlag.

McNamee, S. (2002). The social construction of disorder. In J. D. Raskin and S. K. Bridges (Eds.), *Studies in meaning: Exploring constructivist psychology* (pp. 143–168). New York: Pace University Press.

McNamee, S. (2004). Therapy as social construction: Back to basics and forward toward challenging issues. In T. Strong and D. Pare (Eds.), *Furthering talk: Advances in the discursive therapies* (pp. 253–270). New York: Kluwer Academic/Plenum Press.

McNamee, S. (2009). Postmodern psychotherapeutic ethics: Relational responsibility in practice. *Human Systems, 20*(2), 55–69.

McNamee, S., & Tilsen, J. (2011). *Therapy as social construction: Introduction, clinical consultation, and reflecting team.* Alexandria, VA: Microtraining/Alexander Street Press.

McPhail, B. A. (2004). Questioning gender and sexuality boundaries: What queer theorists, transgendered individuals, and sex researchers can teach social work. *Journal of Gay and Lesbian Social Services, 17*(1), 3–21.

Miller, T. (2001). *Sportsex.* Philadelphia: Temple University Press.

Monk, G., Winslade, J., & Sinclair, S. (2008). *New horizons in multicultural counseling.* Los Angeles: Sage.

Moraga, C., & Anzaldua, G. (Eds.) (1983). *This bridge called my back: Writings by radical women of color.* New York: Haworth Press.

Morrow, D. (2004). Social work practice with gay, lesbian, bisexual and transgender adolescents. *Familes in Society, 85*(1), 91–99.

Munoz, J. E. (1999). *Disidentifications: Queers of color and the performance of politics.* Minneapolis: University of Minnesota Press.

Myerhoff, B. (1978). *Number our days.* New York: Simon & Schuster.

Myerhoff, B. (1982). Life history among the elderly: Performance, visibility, and remembering. In J. Ruby (Ed.), *A crack in the mirror: Reflexive perspectives in anthropology* (pp. 99–117). Philadelphia: University of Pennsylvania Press.

Myerhoff, B. (1986). Life not death in Venice: Its second life. In V. Turner & E. Bruner (Eds.), *The anthropology of experience* (pp. 261–286). Chicago: University of Illinois Press.

Nylund D. (2007). Reading Harry Potter: Popular culture, queer theory, and the fashioning of youth identity. *Journal of Systemic Therapies, 26*(2), 13–24.

Ortner, S. B., & Whitehead, H. (Eds.) (1981). *Sexual meanings: The cultural construction of gender and sexuality.* Cambridge: Cambridge University Press.

Padgug, R. A. (1979). On conceptualizing sexuality in history. *Radical history review, 20*, 3–23.

Parker, I. (1989). Discourse and power. In J. Shotter & K. J. Gergen, (Eds.), *Texts of identity* (pp. 56–69). London: Sage.

Parker, I. (2005). *Qualitative psychology: Introducing radical research.* Maidenhead, England: Open University Press.

Patton, C. (1996). *Fatal advice: How safe-sex education went wrong.* Durham: Duke University Press.

Penn, P. (1982). Circular questioning. *Family Process, 21*, 267–280.

Perel, E. (2006). *Mating in captivity: Unlocking erotic intelligence.* New York: Harper.

Quiroga, J. (2003). From republic to empire: The loss of gay studies. *GLQ: A Journal of Lesbian and Gay Studies, 10*(1), 133–137.

Rabinow, P. (1984). Introduction. In P. Rabinow (Ed.), *The Foucault reader* (pp. 3–29). New York: Pantheon Books.

Rich, A. (1986). *Blood, bread, and poetry: Selected prose, 1979–1985.* New York: Norton.

Rubin, G. (1984). Thinking sex: Notes for a radical theory of the politics of sexuality. In C. S. Vance (Ed.), *Pleasure and danger: Exploring female sexuality* (pp. 267–319). Boston: Routledge.

Rubin, L. C. (Ed.). (2008). *Popular culture in counseling, psychotherapy, and play-based interventions*. New York: Springer Publications.

Russell, S., & Carey, M. (2002). Re-membering: Responding to commonly asked questions. *The International Journal of Narrative Therapy and Community Work, 3*, 23–31.

Ryan, C., & Futterman, D. (1998). *Lesbian and gay youth: Care and counseling*. New York: Columbia University Press.

Ryle, G. (1949). *The concept of mind*. London: Hutchinson.

Saewyc, E., Bearinger, L., Blum, R., & Resnick. M. (1999). Sexual intercourse, abuse and pregnancy among adolescent women: Does sexual orientation make a difference? *Family Planning Perspectives, 31*, 127–131.

Saewyc, E. M., Poon, C. S., Homma, Y., & Skay, C. L. (2008). Stigma management? The links between enacted stigma and teen pregnancy trends among gay, lesbian, and bisexual students in British Columbia. *Canadian Journal of Human Sexuality, 17*(3), 123–139.

Sampson, E. E. (1989). Deconstruction of the self. In J. Shotter & K. J. Gergen (Eds.), *Texts of identity* (pp. 1–19). London: Sage.

Sampson, E. E. (2008). *Celebrating the other: A dialogic account of human nature*. Chagrin Falls, OH: Taos Institute Publication. (Originally published in 1993.)

Savin-Williams, R. (1990). *Gay and lesbian youth: Expressions of identity*. Washington DC: Hemisphere Publishing Corp.

Savin-Williams, R. (1998). . . . *And then I became gay: Young men's stories*. New York: Routledge.

Savin-Williams, R. (2001). *Mom, Dad. I'm gay: How families negotiate coming out*. Washington, DC: APA Press.

Savin-Williams, R. (2005). *The new gay teenager*. Cambridge: Harvard University Press.

Savin-Williams, R., & Cohen, K. M. (Eds.). (1996). *The lives of lesbians, gays, and bisexuals: Children to adults*. Fort Worth: Harcourt Brace.

Savin-Williams, R., & Diamond, L. (1997). Sexual orientation as a developmental context for lesbians, gays, and bisexuals: Biological perspectives. In N. L. Segal, G. E. Weisfeld, & C. C. Weisfeld (Eds.), *Uniting psychology and biology: Integrative perspectives on human development* (pp. 217–238). Washington, DC: APA Press.

Searle, J. (1969). *An essay in the philosophy of language*. Cambridge: Cambridge University Press.

Sedgwick, E. (1990). *Epistemology of the closet*. Berkeley: University of California Press.

Sedgwick, E. (1993). *Tendencies*. Durham: Duke University Press.

Seidman, S. (1993). Identity and politics in a "postmodern" gay culture: Some historical and conceptual notes. In M. Warner (Ed.), *Fear of a queer planet: Queer politics and social theory* (pp. 105–142). Minneapolis: University of Minnesota Press.

Selvini-Palazzoli, M., Boscolo, L., Cecchin, G. & Prata, G. (1980). Hypothesizing-circularity-neutrality: Three guidelines for the conductor of the session. *Family Process, 19*, 3–12.

Shotter, J. (1989). Social accountability and the social construction of "you." In J. Shotter & K. Gergen, (Eds.), *Texts of identity* (pp. 133–151). London: Sage.

Shotter, J. (1990). The social construction of remembering and forgetting. In D. Middleton & D. Edwards (Eds.), *Collective remembering* (pp. 120–138). London: Sage.

Shotter, J. (2003). The social construction of remembering and forgetting. In M. Gergen & K. J. Gergen (Eds.), *Social construction: A reader* (pp. 132–137). Los Angeles: Sage.

Smith, B. (1977). Towards a black feminist criticism. *Conditions, 2*, 25–44.

Spivak, G. (1988). Subaltern studies: Deconstructing histiographies. In R. Guha & G. Spivak (Eds.), *Selected subaltern studies* (pp. 3–34). Oxford: Oxford University Press.

Sullivan, L. (2008). Calvin and Hobbes to the rescue! The therapeutic use of comic strips and cartoons. In L. C. Rubin (Ed.), *Popular culture in counseling, psychotherapy, and play-based interventions* (pp. 43–58). New York: Springer Publications.

Sycamore, M. B. (2008). There's more to life than platinum: Challenging the tyranny of sweatshop-produced rainbow flags and participatory patriarchy. In, M.B. Sycamore, *That's revolting! Queer strategies for resisting assimilation (rev.)* (pp. 1–7). Brooklyn: Soft Skull Press.

Talburt, S. (2004). Constructions of LGBT youth: Opening up subject positions. *Theory into Practice, 43*(2), 116–121.

Thomas, C. (Ed.). (2000). *Straight with a twist*. Urbana, IL: University of Illinois Press.

Tiefer, L. (2004). *Sex is not a natural act* (2nd ed.). Boulder, CO: Perseus.

Tilsen, J., & Nylund, D. (2009). Popular culture texts and young people: Making meaning, honoring resistance, and becoming Harry Potter. *International Journal of Narrative Therapy and Community Work, 2*, 3–10.

Tilsen, J. & Nylund, D. (2010). Homonormativity and queer youth resistance. In L. Moon (Ed.), *Counselling ideologies: Queer challenges to heteronormativity* (pp. 93–104). London: Ashgate.

Tilsen, J., & Nylund, D. (2012). *iYouth: Pop culture, kids, and counseling*. Alexandria, VA.: Microtraining/Alexander Street Press.

Tomm, K. (1987). Interventive interviewing: Part II. Reflexive questioning as a means to enable self-healing. *Family Process, 26*, 167–183.

Tomm, K. (1988). Interventive interviewing: Part III. Intending to ask lineal, circular, strategic or reflexive questions? *Family Process, 27*, 1–15.

Tomm, K., Hoyt, M., & Madigan, S. (1998). Honoring our internalized others and the ethics of caring: A conversation with Karl Tomm. In M. Hoyt (Ed.) *The handbook of constructive therapies* (pp. 198–218). San Francisco: Jossey-Bass.

Troiden, R. R. (1979). Becoming homosexual: A model of identity acquisition. *Psychiatry, 42*, 288–299.

Warner, M. (1991). Introduction: Fear of a queer planet. *Social Text, 9*, 3–17.

Warner, M. (Ed.). (1993). *Fear of a queer planet*. Minneapolis: University of Minnesota Press.

Warner, M. (1999). *The trouble with normal: Sex, politics, and the ethics of queer life*. Cambridge: Harvard University Press.

Weeks, J. (1981). *Sex, politics, and society: The regulation of sexuality since 1800*. London: Longman.

Welle, D. L., Fuller, S. S., Maul, D., Clatts, M. C. (2006). The invisible body of queer youth: Identity and health in the margins of lesbian and trans communities. In A. P. Aragon, (Ed.), *Challenging lesbian norms: Intersex, transgender, intersectional, and queer perspectives* (pp. 43–71). New York: Harrington Park Press.

Westerfelhaus, R., & Lacroix, C. (2006). Seeing "straight" through queer eye: Exposing the strategic rhetoric of heteronormativity in a mediated ritual of gay rebellion. *Critical Studies in Media Communication, 23*(5), 426–444.

White, M. (1988). Saying hullo again: The incorporation of the lost relationship in the resolution of grief. *Dulwich centre newsletter*, spring, 7–11.

White, M. (1995). *Re-authoring lives: Interviews and essays*. Adelaide, AU: Dulwich Centre Publications.

White, M. (2007). *Maps of narrative practice*. New York: Norton.

White, M., & Epston, D. (1990). *Narrative means to therapeutic ends*. New York: Norton.

Wilchins, R. (2002). Queerer bodies. In J. Nestle, C. Howell, & R. Wilchins (Eds.), *Genderqueer: Voices from beyond the sexual binary* (pp. 33–46). Los Angeles: Alyson Books.

Wilchins, R. (2004). *Queer theory, gender theory: An instant primer*. Los Angeles: Alyson Books.

Wittgenstein, L. (1953). *Philosophical investigations*. (Anscombe, G.E.M., Trans.). Oxford: Basil Blackwell.

Index

About the Author

Julie Tilsen, PhD, is the training director for the International Center for Clinical Excellence (www.centerforclinicalexcellence.com) and an associate of the Taos Institute (www.taosinstitute.net). Her work is featured in several counselor training videos produced by Alexander Street Press including: *Queer Theory in Action: Theoretical Resources for Therapeutic Conversations* (parts 1 and 2); *Feedback Informed Treatment; Therapy as Social Construction*; and *iYouth: Kids, Counseling, and Pop Culture*. Julie's work focuses on conversational practices anchored in socially just approaches and an ethic of relational responsiveness. Julie loves living in Minneapolis with her partner Lauri, where the bike culture, food culture, and women's hockey culture are most awesome.